THE DEVELOPMENTAL LOGIC OF

SOCIAL SYSTEMS

Volume 60, Sage Library of Social Research

Sage Library of Social Research

The DEVELOPMENTAL LOGIC of SOCIAL SYSTEMS

Henry Teune
Zdravko Mlinar

Volume 60
SAGE LIBRARY OF
SOCIAL RESEARCH

SAGE PUBLICATIONS   Beverly Hills   London

For information address:

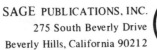 

SAGE PUBLICATIONS, INC.   SAGE PUBLICATIONS LTD
275 South Beverly Drive   28 Banner Street
Beverly Hills, California 90212   London EC1Y 8QE

Printed in the United States of America

Library of Congress Cataloging in Publication Data

Teune, Henry.
 The developmental logic of social systems.

 (Sage library of social research ; v. 60)
 1. Social change. 2. Social systems. 3. Economic
development. I. Mlinar, Zdravko, joint author. II. Title
HN28.T48   301.24   77-26099
ISBN 0-8039-0900-4
ISBN 0-8039-0901-2 pbk.

FIRST PRINTING

CONTENTS

PREFACE

Concern about development is an historically explainable phenomenon. Secular interpretations of societal developmental processes are confined largely to the nineteenth and twentieth centuries when rapid changes provided visible relief to the past. These massive changes occurred primarily in Europe and North America. They clearly appeared to be more than repetitions of past experience. Because of these macrodevelopmental changes, theories rapidly accumulated empirical referents.

With the inclusion of the rest of the world into the international system of independent states and with revolutionary changes in several established European and Asian countries after World War II, the focus of developmental studies shifted its emphasis from older industrialized countries to these newly formed systems. Although almost all these societies had undergone change, the most decisive came about as a result of the establishment and collapse of Western empires and through the emergence of a new world order that encompassed more than 100 countries rather than a few dominant ones. Recent changes have been so far reaching that nearly half of the people living today have experienced at least one, however nominal, discontinuous change in the system in which they live.

These remarks are made to convey our awareness of the relationship between this theory of development and the world in which we live. This analysis, we believe, could not have aspired to be as global or as general if it were done a few decades ago. The diversity of developmental phenomena was either not present or not coded as relevant to general analysis. Further, only in the past two or three decades have most social scientists become aware that their developmental "models" were founded on limited experience, resulting in parochial views. The debate over implicit development models has led, to some extent, to the abandonment of theory in favor of idiographic descriptions of particular developmental experiences. We believe, however, that such diversity is a challenge to even broader theory, whatever the risk of a new parochialism.

We began working together in the summer of 1965 in a four country empirical study on leadership and change at the local level, the final report of which was completed in 1969. One of the by-products of this research was a large range of data on change at the local level. Between 1965 and 1969 at various times, we assumed the responsibility of attempting to place this research in a broader theoretical context. The force of the circumstances in such a demanding international research project made this task nearly impossible in the time allowed. During this time, however, we did attempt to deal with specific local manifestations of development, such as urbanization and community integration, and we accumulated fragmentary notes on the problems of change at the local level, especially the linkages of the local unit to the broader system of which it is a part.

In 1968 we decided to take our theoretical efforts outside of the specific context of this research project. We proposed a broad-ranging analysis of social change at the local level applying data to certain models of change. In the fall of 1969, after an extensive analysis of change at the communal level in Slovenia, we made a decision to write a book on "theories" of development.

After our decision to write this book we drafted two long chapters on "Developmental Change." The first was an overview of approaches to the study of development and change. The second defined development in terms of social space. The concept of social space and its relationship to physical space gave our theory an empirical orientation to local systems. The second chapter elaborated those processes which "expanded" social space across a defined physical space, such as the exchange of goods, mobility, and accumulation of resources.

In the summer of 1971 we had an opportunity to work together again for about three weeks, a year and a half after the first two chapters were written. What became clear was the theoretical gulf between developmental phenomena, such as urbanization, industrialization, or generally "modernization," concepts referring to specific spatial-temporal manifestations of developmental change, and general properties of social systems, such as scale, integration, and complexity. We checked this out by making an inventory of several hundred developmental concepts from a variety of publications on development. Most literature on development dealt with historical manifestations of development rather than with development as a general social process. We concluded that theoretical advances would be hampered as long as the focus was these manifestations rather than the central question: why development? We decided that what we had written earlier was phenomenological and would best be discarded in favor of a more general approach.

In 1972 a Fulbright grant and a sabbatical year for one of the authors and an academic leave of absence for the other made possible a longer period of intensive work. At this time we began to present a number of papers on our thinking in order to obtain criticism from others. In March we delivered a paper on "Development and the Openness of the System"; in April, a paper on "Social, Political, and Control Systems,"; in June, "System Choice and System Development"; and in October, "Developmental Perspectives on Local Participation." There was an additional paper on a related topic which we dealt with in a developmental perspective: "The Wealth of Cities and Other Social Values." These papers and the conferences to which they were addressed diverted us from our major task, but they also made us face the problem of clarifying our thinking. In the first paper of 1972, for example, we discussed the concept of social space as development. Then we substantially redefined our concept of development. Many changes were stimulated by these conferences and meetings.

By late summer and early fall of 1972 we had come to the following conclusions about the nature of our work:

(1) that it must be cast in the language of social systems rather than in the context of specific countries or societies;

(2) that it must be truly global, arrogantly perhaps pretending to encompass both the "developed and underdeveloped" countries, past, present, and future;

(3) that it must be consistently disciplined by the question "why development";

(4) that it must be put into a broad historical context, centuries rather than decades and years, and in particular that it must emphasize the future; and

(5) that it must deal with the total system rather than any particular sector of it, such as the polity, the economy, or the society.

During 1973 and 1974 we continued to work on the manuscript and to present papers focusing on some aspects of our thinking on development, which are not included in this volume. Two of these papers were coauthored. The first was the "Concept of Development: Theory and Policy," in June 1973. This was followed by two papers on the value implications of development in July 1973: "Values, Technology and Development" and "Development of Territorial Social Systems: Technology and Freedom in Space and Time." In August 1973 we further elaborated our thinking with, "Alternative Local Political Organizations in Development" (with J. J. Wiatr); in December, "Developmental Change: Theory and Policy." Two papers focused again on the local level were presented at the International Sociological Association, "Ecological Factors and Social Development Theory" and "Development and Territorial Political Systems." The opportunities to present these papers publicly enabled us to relate some of our ideas to the concerns and languages of others.

The completion of the manuscript was delayed by a decision in 1975 to organize an International Workshop on the "Comparative Ecological Analysis of Social Change" in Ljubljana in August 1976. One purpose of this workshop was to link our theoretical concern about space, social organization, and development to an on-going area of empirical research—social ecology. Such a linkage was, in our view, imperative to avoid theoretical writing devoid of empirical and practical concerns.

In the summer of 1975, one of the authors got a fellowship from the U.S. National Academy of Sciences, a proposal was written and funds sought. Two additional papers bringing our theoretical statements more closely to an area of empirical research in political science were presented in September to the International Political Science Association Committee on Local Government and Politics Workshop (in Helsinki) on "Linkages Between the Center and Local Levels of Government," "Development and National-Local Linkages" (Mlinar), and "Information, Control, and National-Local Linkages" (Teune).

In the summer of 1976, the workshop on "Comparative Ecological Analysis of Social Change" was convened as part of the International Sociological Association's Committee on Social Ecology's program of activities. Its primary intellectual purpose was to redefine classical social ecology so that it would become relevant to the general theoretical concerns of development and change. By bringing cross-national and cross-temporal data to this workshop, it was hoped that the narrower concepts in social ecology, such as density, concentration, competition, succession, and the like could be incorporated into more general theoretical perspectives on developmental change.

During the workshop on "Comparative Ecological Analysis of Social Change," we presented papers relating development to social ecology: "Development and the Social Ecology of Developmental Change" (Mlinar et al.), which involved an analysis of data on Slovenian communes and "The Developmental Ecology of Political Intervention" (Teune), which pointed to specific cross-national and cross-time data to test some specific propositions about local governments derived from the theory. These papers, with other workshop papers, are now being published.

Many of these ideas, of course, were presented in classes and other forums of criticism. One such was the workshop on "Elites and Political Decision-Making in Chinese History" held at the University of Pennsylvania in June 1976 and sponsored by the American Council of Learned Societies. This was a unique opportunity to test ideas against a group of young historians who, perhaps more than any other, have the time frame of centuries and indeed millenia to which our theory aspires.

Although both of us have research experience in countries other than our own, we do not consider ourselves experts on any particular area of the world. Also, relative independence from associations with particular groups working directly on development has made us conscious of taking risks in departing from the standards of previous, established publications. Although as social scientists we owe a debt to both the classical and modern thinkers on development, change, and economic growth, we have made a conscious effort to focus on our own ideas rather than to review and reinterpret those of others. Accordingly, we have avoided citations in the text.

One of us has been identified with the discipline of sociology and, in particular, with the sociology of the local communities; the other with various aspects of political science and, from time to time, with the methodology of social research. Our involvement in the international research project on local leadership solidified our commitment to a comparative approach to social research. We have both been involved in research in our own countries as well as in Asia. We have formulated these ideas, therefore, in a general, comparative language rather than in a way suited to improve understanding about specific countries or specific disciplinary concerns.

This book is written for professional social scientists interested in social change in general and development in particular. There are only a few examples or arguments that a particular case fits the theory or some aspects of the theory. The focus is on classes or types of cases.

This manuscript was written in the middle of the United Nation's Decade of Development. At this time of increased interest in development on the part of political leaders around the world, doubts are emerging about the possibility of development. Most discussions of development in the nineteenth and twentieth centuries were dominated by economic growth and its consequent economic and social inequalities. Within the last few decades basic questions about development as economic growth have arisen—its definition, its limited time horizon, its sectorial narrowness, its desirability, and its feasibility? These questions have not only stimulated a reassessment of the value of economic growth but also cautious policies: population control; conservation of resources; restriction on the use of space; and regulation of the environment. Thus during the Decade of Development there are renewed efforts to attain rapid economic growth by poor countries, while wealthy countries center their concern on the undesirable long term effects of economic growth.

The paradox is that the economically developed countries are struggling to cope with the consequences of economic growth, and in some cases to prevent further growth; economically undeveloped countries are struggling to achieve a goal discounted by others. This paradox has contributed to intellectual confusion in discussions of development.

One response to this confusion is to broaden the meaning of development by extending it to sectors other than economic: political development, institutional development, urban development, regional development. Another response is to broaden development by extension to the future—projecting current tendencies into the twenty-first century.

Our approach is neither to divide development into particular sectors nor to project existing trends, but to take into account whole social systems, structural change, and the past and present as well as the future. Such an approach can give new meaning to the concept of development and thus reorient research on development to the problems of structural change.

Philadelphia, 1977   *Henry Teune*

Ljubljana, 1977   *Zdravko Mlinar*

INTRODUCTION

This book addresses the most perplexing theoretical problem in the social sciences: the explanation of social change. Whatever the historical interpretation, there is little doubt that twentieth century societies have achieved unprecedented scale. Why this has occurred is the focus of this theoretical analysis.

Scale is development; increases in the scale of social systems is developmental change; and increases in scale are more than simple increases in size or quantity. Increases in scale determine both the nature of the actors and their relationships, which determine the scale of the system. This is the basic logic of developmental change.

Structural Explanation

Broadly speaking, there are three secular types of explanations of increasing scale. First, there are explanations founded on man, his knowledge, will, and purpose. Human resources and technology are central to explaining change. Second, there are explanations derived from random processes, by which new elements, autonomously discovered or imposed, are introduced, diffused, and adapted to. These random processes explain the survival of some societies and the demise of others. Third, there are explanations based on the logic of social systems. Each social system has a structure of relationships which influences its future course of development.

This theory of development is an explication of the logic of social systems that causes or drives them to develop. It does not deal directly with either subjective factors or random processes.

There is a logic to social systems that generates new components and changes their relationships. The "Developmental Logic of Social Systems" explains change as an autonomous force, as a dynamic. This perhaps is the most difficult type of theoretical explanation of change, because change is seen as deriving from complex interactions rather than from the behavior of identifiable actors.

The history of any social system, however, is only partially a consequence of its logic. People do have will and purposes; "accidental" discoveries are critical. To explain the historical state of any particular social system, it is necessary to take into account both human and random variations. Not to do so would result in an incomplete explanation.

But despite the importance of human purpose, the structure of the system remains a theoretical problem. Without an understanding of the logic or structure of social systems, it is not possible to explain why a particular political system and its leaders or a particular technological discovery made a difference. The logic of the system in which human actions occur is a decisive condition for understanding their impact on the system.

Since the social system is the decisive context, a theory that explains it is more general than other types of exploration. The social system is often ignored in the face of the attractions of the particulars of a political movement or a great inventor. Although only one part of an explanation of the complexity of a specific system, it is nonetheless requisite for understanding the others. The longer the time perspective on change, the more the logic of social systems acquires explanatory power, diminishing the importance of specific historical events.

Theoretical Generality

The study of development must be macrohistorical, and macro-comparative. It confronts social scientists with the greatest amount of variance to be explained—all countries, subsystems of countries —past, present, and future. It requires an orientation to generality. This very challenge has given impetus to recent arguments that development as a theoretical and a research focus in social science should be abandoned in favor of more delimited problems.

Despite the easy but valid criticisms that development theory is vacuous generality, the point of departure of this discussion is that most development theory is too phenomenological and particularistic. It is phenomenological in the sense that it is directed to explaining urbanization, industrialization, mechanization, etc., rather than to seeing these as manifestations of development, which is more general and basic to all complex social systems. It is particularistic in the sense that it deals with problems in specific settings (such as elections in systems with party competition, economic growth under conditions of a market economy, and even agricultural extension services). Such theories apply to specific circumstances that are not delineated by general and comparable concepts. Specific, however, does not mean precisely defined. In some cases, the specific circumstances, "Poland after 1945" or "India after independence," are more imprecise than general theoretical concepts, such as standardization or predictability.

By emphasizing generality, it is possible to overcome some of the problems and criticisms of existing developmental theories. This emphasis has costs in terms of other criteria of a "good" theory. For social theories in the process of becoming definitive, such trade offs may be unavoidable. The most obvious of these is that between generality and precision or accuracy of prediction. Specific predictions from this theory can be made, but they will be predictions in the context of the theory—consonant and consistent with the theory concerning classes of phenomena—rather than orthodox predictions which are strictly reproducible deductions from the theory with respect to concrete cases.

The implications of an emphasis on generality are several. First, generality requires a macrosystem perspective on systems of some inclusiveness—countries rather than cities, societies rather than families, regions rather than villages. One direct consequence of this is concern with multiple levels within the system, "subsystems" of greater and lesser inclusiveness. Indeed, this is one of the two basic developmental dynamics in this analysis—the continual shift of activities to levels of greater and greater inclusiveness and complexity.

Second, generality requires a comparative approach covering many systems, and, optimally, all systems. The only way it is possible to study general developmental processes and their impact is to examine variations in development across all systems. Not all societies composed of human beings develop. Those that develop, i.e., characterized by the logic of development, are the social systems to which this theory is addressed.

Third, generality requires a long term historical view. In terms of generality, a "good" theory of development would not only be able to explain basic characteristics of all existing systems, but also all systems of the past and future. Developmental theories often juxtapose historical and comparative cases where the present and future of less developed systems are interpreted in terms of the recent past of developed systems. Few embrace the future of both the most and the least developed. A general theory of development ought, however, to cover the past, present, and future of systems at all levels of development. This means a time frame of generations and centuries rather than of regimes or decades.

Fourth, generality requires an orientation to basic social processes rather than those indicative of change. The distinction between fundamental factors and their manifestations must be contextually defined in terms of both the generality of the theory and the conditions of particular cases. One basic relationship among people involves their relationship to private property; a derived manifestation of this is the distribution of horses and agricultural land. This does not mean that what is not basic is not decisive for behavior in a specific context. On the contrary, what is derived is often crucial. In this theory, for example, the rate of innovation is a necessary factor for explaining increasing variety. To say that innovation contributes to an increase in variety is a near-tautology. Innovation is derived, however, from a set of other basic conditions. These conditions stimulate innovations and their absorption which in turn accelerates the rate of development; innovation acts as a derived accelerator. Distinctions between basic and derived factors are central to this theory, whose focus is on the dynamics of developmental change.

Fifth, generality requires a "wholistic" rather than a sectorial framework. The general dynamics that interact to create change must be considered together rather than isolated as economic, political, or social change. One of the dominant features of development is the differentiation of sectors and their absorption. This macrotheory will explain the emergence of sectors and the conditions under which they will merge.

Sixth, generality calls for a theoretical interpretation of specific historical events. Rather than limiting analysis to "Sweden" or "France," defined in terms of historical peculiarities, it is necessary to translate these specific historical configurations into general properties of systems, such as systems of late industrialization or systems with a "memory" of conflictive stratification, in order to compare any system with another or all other systems. Such historical factors will be translated into general theoretical terms.

The emphasis on generality places this theory in the tradition of "grand" sociological theory. It has been argued, however, that "middle range" theories are preferable because specific hypotheses are more transparent and, thus, are more vulnerable to disconfirmation. "Grand theory" is seen as too general and, consequently, vague, imprecise, and not unconfirmable.

A strict trade-off between specific and testable and general and not testable theory is not defensible. All theories, regardless of their level of generality, are by definition made up of general statements. In order to test them, measurement systems are required to relate the general concepts to specific cases. On the one hand, it could be argued that the grand developmental theorists were too phenomenological, too specific about money, bureaucracy, religion, and the like; and, on the other hand, too removed from the measurement problems of relating theory to more than selected examples. Testability is a question of measurement systems rather than the level of generality of the theory.

The general concepts of this theory will be made partially "operational" by pointing to classes of phenomena to which concepts refer rather than describing specific instances of their occurrence. A measurement system for development will be outlined. In this way, hopefully, the gap between the power of generality and the precision of specificity can at least be described. For example, the time-cost-distance function is one factor that affects interdependence among the components of a system. Urbanization or urban areas manifest a low time-cost-distance constraint on access to variety. Another example is the transfer of variety from individuals to the system or collectivity; total mechanization of certain activities, such as water supply, is a manifestation of such transfers.

Although the primary theoretical thrust is generality, that is, properties and their interrelationships across all social systems, at all levels, and for all periods of time, development will be discussed at four different levels of generality, the lowest level of which is suggestive of measurement operations. First, there is the logic of developmental change. These are "law-like" statements, which, once present in empirical systems, take on the reality of dynamics. An example is the law of aggregative diversity which states that the larger the number of properties of specific components, the greater the probability that that component will be different from all other components of the system and the greater the probability that that component will share properties with other components. These laws spell out, in effect, the dynamics of developmental change. Following from these dynamics are a few derived factors which affect the nature of the laws themselves, such as the greater the variety of components (along with some other things), the greater the probability of innovation, which in turn affects the rate of increase in the variety of a system.

Second, there are basic social activities, such as production, consumption, and distribution. These are fundamental aspects of individual and group activities that affect social change. In order for there to be any development, there must be production. But these activities are less general than the developmental dynamics. Their role in development is conditioned by the overall rate and level of development. Whether production and consumption are separate social functions will depend on the level of development. Whether consumption is a negative factor in development, detracting from savings and investment, or a positive one, stimulating production and investment, depends, again, on the level of development of a system.

The remaining two levels of generality have specific developmental manifestations. The third is developmental processes, changes over time in the characteristics of the activities of the components of a system, such as their rationalization and standardization. These are properties of production, consumption, and other basic social activities. Standardization increases as development proceeds. Such developmental processes themselves are preconditions for further developmental change. Although they do not occur independently of development, political decisions may accelerate them.

Finally, there are phenomenological manifestations of development, such as the general contemporary ones labelled "modernization," which include industrialization and urbanization, or the conventional indicators of "development," such as education, hospital beds, and retail trade. Most developmental studies have both begun and ended here, obscuring the basic dynamics of developmental change. From a general theoretical perspective, education and urbanization are specific historical manifestations of development and, thus, are inappropriate indicators of development both for social systems of low complexity or of higher development than the industrialized countries that have served as the primary examples of development in recent decades.

These phenomenological manifestations are indicators of development and must be interpreted in the context of specific systems, especially the developmental context. Measuring development with universalistic indicators, such as per capita income, must give way to contextually defined indicators.

A general theoretical orientation enforces the discipline of the question why: Why change? Why development? This question, however, leads to an infinite regress of inquiry which must stop in favor of some answers, relegating other questions to assumptions. But often these assumptions are the potential core of a more general theory. In contrast to the "why" orientation that forces theoretical generality, many theories of development explicate or descriptively summarize the process of change. Education leads to rising expectations; rising expectations, unless they are fulfilled, lead to frustration, frustration leads to disenchantment with the system, etc. Or, the politicization of the population proceeds at a more rapid rate than institutionalization, which, at a certain point leads to political instability and the decay of the political system. Such formulations of connections and sequences do not directly deal with the question of why: Why does education lead to increased expectations? Why are these expectations focused on the system rather than on individual success and failure?

Furthermore, such relationships as those between education and frustration are not at a high level of generality, no matter how well they may fit as descriptors of university students in Latin America or workers in Europe.

This evaluation contrasts the general theoretical approach with others. A specific critique of other theories of change, however, will be avoided. Usually such comments distort in order to make a point. The best commentary is the well articulated and argued alternative. The advantages of this theory are pinned to the power of generality. The generality aspired to, of course, builds on the theories of others, and these intellectual debts are obvious in most cases.

Systemic Interpretation

A general and structural theoretical approach to development must be systemic. This theory is formulated in the language of systems. Development is a property of all social systems of some level of complexity and, as a property of systems, it must be expressed in the language of systems. But once this is said, there remain several alternative languages of systems. The focus in our theoretical discourse will be complex social systems.

Complex systems are those that have many components and levels of components rather than a few, and many different types of interdependences among the components rather than a few. Although this definition is imprecise, it excludes several types of "systems," such as dyads, formal decision-making bodies, and interpersonal conflict systems. Developmental systems are complex. They are defined by autonomous change in relationships among components and in the nature of the components themselves. But all complex systems are not necessarily developmental.

"System" is a logical concept or a general paradigm referring to components and their interactions over time, including feedback. "Systems theories" would be those using the logical form of a systems paradigm to express relationships. Theory must be specified in terms of concepts, rules for empirically interpreting those concepts, relationships, etc. There are no system theories per se but rather theories expressed in one of the various systems languages. A systems logic is used in this developmental theory, not a systems theory.

First, a systems approach views causes as dynamics. Causes of development emerge from, or are derived from, the interactions of several factors or variables over time. This view of cause contrasts with the search for casual agents or factors expressed as independent and dependent variables. In this theory, for example, developmental change occurs because the variety of the components interacts with the variety of the system, and the variety of the system is derived from the diversity of its components. This interaction leads to change at the system level, which in turn leads to changes at the component level.

Second, a system approach to social systems requires that individuals be connected to the system. But because this theory is systemic, these connections must be explained. They will also be minimized. Individuals will be brought into the systems through certain laws of individual behavior that have direct implications for the system. Some of the primary structures of the dynamics of developmental change, for example, are the differences between individuals and the system. The system can increase its variety almost infinitely, but individual members of the system have a finite capacity for variety, resulting in system level responses, such as distribution. One aspect of developmental dynamics will be system laws clashing with the laws of individual behavior. Another basic connection is that individuals prefer variety, leading to conflict and competition.

Third, a system approach addresses change over time. By definition, the components of systems interact over time and change the state of the system. Although theories of change may be directed to explaining differences between two or more points in time, a "proper" theory of change ought to provide for the derivation of change coefficients, the rate of change, from the theoretical statements themselves; it ought to predict changes in the rate of change. In addition, a theory of change ought also to explain qualitative changes or transformations in the nature of the system. The theory to be presented does, for example, explain why the level of development predicts changes in the rate of development and also qualitative transformations in the social system, both of the nature of the components and the relationships within the system.

Fourth, a system dynamic approach implies a system closed to external factors that induce change. The focus is change intrinsic to social systems itself—why development would occur in a social system if it were the only social system in the world. Such an approach excludes critical historical events, such as world wars, international demonstration effects, and external forces. These must, however, be considered in any explanation of the development of any specific system. A systems approach ought to state the dynamics of developmental change and treat other factors as random or disturbing events. "Resources," "people," and "neighbors," for example, are treated as exogeneous in this theory. Although all theoretical systems are, by definition, closed, that is, they consider only the factors that are stated in the theory and no others, all empirical systems are in fact open to external influences.

The degree to which systems are influenced by factors not discussed can be described as the openness of the system. But openness must itself be explained. It can be predicted, from the system's state of development. Openness then can be used to describe one system fading away in favor of more encompassing systems. This shift in levels is a process intrinsic to the development dynamics of social systems.

Fifth, a system approach to development as a process intrinsic to the system requires the use of a positive rather than a negative feedback paradigm. Positive feedback systems are those that change as a result of previous changes. In this theory, analysis is focused on changes in the relationships among the components. Negative feedback systems, of which control systems are perhaps the most well-understood, treat "change" as deviations from prescribed goal states, which may occur either as a result of processes internal to the system or of action external to it. They are analyzed in terms of such properties as stability and equilibrium. Positive feedback languages are poorly understood, although they are obviously useful for constructing social theory and for understanding complex social systems. Negative feedback logics are well understood, and are useful for specific theories of formal social organizations and, especially, economic and political ones. They have limited utility for complex social systems.

Value Implications

Development and developmental change have consequences that are both "desirable and undesirable," depending on the context of a particular social system and on how classes, groups, and individuals are affected by it. As will be discussed, development will, under certain circumstances, increase inequality and stimulate conflict, just as it can enhance individual freedom of choice. Thus development in value terms should be viewed as instrumental; it is a general property of a social system that serves other values, and, accordingly, cannot be taken as being universally and intrinsically desirable except perhaps in the very long run. Insofar as human freedom and the possibility for the development of the human personality are concerned, the assumption of this theory is that on balance development as defined is desirable, if not for one generation, then for future generations.

Second, development as a process of change raises the issues of single or multiple paths and developmental end states. As development is a general property of social systems, there is a variety of specific ways whereby particular social and political systems can increase their scale. As the end point of development is a global system, the question of a variety of possible end states is logically impossible. The global system will, by theoretical definition, encompass all the variety in the world and make it accessible to all individuals. In any event, the empirical test of this theoretical prediction is beyond the life-time of this generation.

Third, there always is the issue of whose interests a theory serves. Does it create quiescence among the deprived or objectively poor? does it stimulate action for immediate change? does it aid interests in the status quo? This theory is secular, that is, it is embodied in the empirical rather than an extra-mundane world, defining what is "good." As such, it can be used either to foster developmental change or to preserve the status quo.

Fourth, there is the issue of determinism and historical necessity. The design of the theory presupposes certain laws of social change. The discovery and confirmation of such laws is the goal of social inquiry. These laws state the conditions under which certain changes will, or are likely to, occur. The existence of such laws, however, neither implies iron "historical" laws that predict inevitable outcomes for every, or indeed any case, nor precludes choice to use these laws to achieve radically different outcomes. A clear distinction must be made between the existence of social laws, a term with strong connotations, and predicting or explaining particular cases. There are conditions that must obtain before these laws can take effect. These conditions are variable across cases, and indeed, even a strong law may have only one or a few cases directly manifesting it. Also, such "laws" are multiple, that is they operate empirically in combinations. Such combinations often produce unique outcomes for particular cases. Furthermore, certain events, even decisive ones, are better explained as random happenings that emerge from the convergence of circumstances that practically could not have been predicted, although once they had "happened" certain consequences might have been predicted, such as Hitler's becoming Chancellor of Germany in 1933 leading to Nazi domination of Europe. Such events may "turn the course of history." Again, a distinction must be made between the presence of general laws and the explanations and predictions that will be unique in every concrete case. Universalistic historical patterns do not follow from universalistic laws.

As mentioned in the preface, the state of the world, and, in particular, the recent history of countries has made it possible to look at developmental change in a broad, comparative and historical context. For many countries the first reasonably accurate data on social characteristics and behavior were gathered in the early 1960s and only in the past decade has there been specific data on changes and events in most of these countries.

As development continues in the near future, there will be a shift of theoretical interest from the particular process in specific countries to global patterns of developmental change. In order for patterns of change to be observed, the system must have a certain level of complexity and interdependence among its components. At the global level, in contrast to the underdeveloped international system, the properties of "systemness" are rudimentary, and hardly worth mentioning. But such a shift to the global level is beginning to become apparent. This theory hopefully is a first step in moving the study of development from the confines of specific countries to the world as a whole.

PART I

THE DYNAMICS OF

DEVELOPMENTAL SYSTEMS

The following chapters present some of the dynamics of developmental change. The first chapter defines social systems and development; the second presents the dynamics of structural changes required for the topic of the third chapter, the integration diversity.

Development is a property of systems, but only of certain classes of systems. Three general types of systems must be distinguished in order to analyze the dynamics of developmental systems: mechanical systems, ecological or growth systems, and developmental systems. Mechanical systems neither generate any new properties nor relationships among their components. Any "item" that is different from that defined is not only disturbing but also disruptive. Ecological or growth systems adapt to their environments, increasing or decreasing the number of their components in response to their environment, but neither generate new kinds of components nor new relationships. In analyzing either mechanical or ecological systems the concepts of equilibrium and stability rather than of development are intrinsic. Adaptation is the basic dynamic of ecological systems; increases or decreases in size, their response. Inputs are the basic dynamics of closed, mechanical systems; outputs, their response. Developmental systems are defined by their capacity to generate new properties and to integrate them which results in changing the nature of the components and their relationships. It is this type of system, and the dynamics by which it generates variety and integrates it, that is the focus of Part I.

The prototype of the closed system is the machine with its repetitive control behavior, responses to change as deviance to be corrected. The prototypes of ecological systems are biological systems which change to adapt to the environment. The prototypes of developmental systems are social systems. Many social systems, defined as social because their components are human, are not social systems in the sense of being developmental systems, but are, rather, ecological growth systems changing because of their adaptation to their environment, rather than changing autonomously. New items are disturbing to ecological systems, and are, indeed, generally rejected. The dynamics of developmental change do not apply to these systems, which are appropriately analyzed in terms of biological or ecological models of man and his physical environment.

A long-standing criticism of a "systems approach" to social systems is that it tends to be mechanical or biological. This is a sound criticism, but in the development of science it is understandable why better understood systems, simpler and better integrated systems, such as machines or a population of predators, should serve as models for more complex and less well understood systems. This is a proper function of analogies in science.

Part I attempts a direct assault on developmental systems, the prototype of which is a social system which generates new properties which are integrated. A model of developmental social systems could be the most general one against which to understand the nature of both mechanical and biological systems. Once social systems are understood, mechanical and biological systems no longer need to serve as models; rather they, being less complex, are understood in terms of the more complex. To the extent that the logic of developmental systems is understood, the social sciences can be freed from the tyranny of mechanical and biological systems about which so many have complained for so long. The solution to the distortions that result from applying biological and mechanical systems to the social world is not critique but a viable alternative model of complex social systems.

Chapter 1

DEVELOPMENT AND SOCIAL SYSTEMS

Development is the integrated diversity of systems or their scale. Diversity is an aggregative relational property of the components of the system; integration is a property of the interdependencies among components. Diversity and integration are independent properties of a system. Their interaction is one of the basic dynamics of developmental change.

The state of this interaction at any point in time for any system is the basis for assessing its level of development. Development is a quantitative concept; developmental change, a qualitative one. By definition development is a characteristic of all systems with interdependent components. All systems which by definition have interdependent components must have some level of integration of their components, a theoretically defined point rather than a specified quantity. They must also have at least one difference in their components to allow for interdependence.

Concepts and terms that are related to this definition of development include organized complexity for formal organizations, differentiation for societies, and functional integration for groups. These concepts, however, do not explicitly incorporate the dynamic combination of both diversity and integration conveyed by the concept of development.

Developmental change is the change in the nature of the components, or the relationships among them, that results from increases in the level of development. As such, the concept of developmental change is qualitative rather than quantitative.[1] Changes in components are primarily the emergence of levels within the system and their deaggregation. The primary changes in relationships are both in the relationships among components and in the components' relationships to the system. From developmental change a number of more specific changes follow.

Systems

A system is a logical concept having the following minimal defining properties:

(a) at least two elements, which may be defined (e.g., groups) or undefined (e.g., individuals or "empty" logical symbols);

(b) at least one rule of interdependence such that a change in one element leads to a change(s) in the other(s) and those changes in the other component(s) lead to a change in the first; and

(c) at least two points in time during which the interaction or changes take place.

"Systems" are a class of logics or grammars for stating relationships among elements or "things" over time. Systems languages differ from those of sets in that set languages define aggregates of objects or elements that share one or more characteristics. A set language raises the question: what properties do members of this set share? A systems language, in contrast, can express not only shared properties but also connections among properties of the elements over time, even though those properties are not shared. Statistics are the appropriate language of analysis for sets; causal dynamics that for systems.

SYSTEM COMPONENTS

When the elements of a set have the property of interdependence, even if only minimally, the elements of that set become the components of a system. In addition to stating their interdependence, the components must be defined. Except for systems with a small number of individuals as components, such as a dyad, system interpretations of social behavior that define individuals as components are, because of their number, too complex to analyze. Thus most interpretations of social systems use as components aggregates of people (such as urban or rural populations), groups (such as age generations), institutions (such as churches), or slices of behavior of all or some individuals (such as consumers, voters, or investors).

The components that are defined and identified for a social system depend, of course, on many factors, but they should be guided primarily by the purpose of the analysis and the nature of the system being analyzed. A theoretical interpretation of social systems ought, however, to define the components in the language of that theory; and a theory of developmental change ought to state how these components change.

In this theory, the components of a social system are independent of the system in some aspects of their behavior, and in others dependent on the system. The extent to which their behavior is linked to other components, and the system as a whole, varies both among the components and across time. Thus, each component can be assessed in terms of how well integrated it is with the system.

As components of a social system, they acquire, hold, and transfer various kinds of social properties. What properties they possess at one point in time determines their behavior at the next point in time. Furthermore, the components themselves can organize their properties. This organization of properties determines the kinds of relationships the components can have with other components, and will be referred to as the organization of variety.

SYSTEM LEVELS

Social systems can have several kinds of subsystems. A subsystem would be a subset of system components whose behavior in some regards, such as voting or producing, is determined to a greater extent by their membership in that subsystem than by their relationships to other subsystems. For example, an individual's political behavior might be better predicted by his interaction within a trade union than by his interaction outside of it.

Some subsystems will be inclusive of other subsystems. The inclusiveness of subsystems is the basis for defining levels within the system. If the components of a system are totally exclusive, that is, do not incorporate any other components or parts of them, then there are no system levels. The components are structurally, if not behaviorally, equal. If there are several subsystems and some are more or less inclusive of others, then there is at least one additional level, not including the levels of the system itself and the components (two irreducible levels of systems).

There are two meanings of "higher" levels of system. First, there is the aggregative meaning—all of a subset of components defined by a shared property. Any subset plus one additional component would produce a level of aggregation higher than the original set. A second meaning of level is behavioral—the point of higher aggregation implies a difference in behavior. The behavior of the members within the set is different than it would be if it were not a member of that set. In this behavioral rather than aggregative sense of levels, each level is a relatively autonomous subsystem with respect to some domain of behavior. One problem for theoretical analysis is to specify what levels of aggregation constitute these behavior levels within the total system—for empirical analysis the problem is to demonstrate that aggregate levels are behavioral ones.

SYSTEM INTERDEPENDENCIES

All systems, both logical (excluding definitional identities) and empirical, differ with respect to a few general properties: the total number of components, the number of properties of the components, and the strength of the linkages among the components. Simple systems have few components and properties and uniform strength of interdependence, either deterministic or probabilistic. A protean social system of two people, for example, linked in such a way that a change in one would lead to a change in the other over two points in time embodies the minimal defining characteristics of a system.[2] This is a two component, two property, one linkage, and one "act" system. It is a closed, deterministic, nonfeedback system.

Complex systems, in contrast, whether logical or empirical,

contain a variety of types of components, properties, and relationships. Developmental systems are complex, with the additional critical factor that their components, properties, and relationships change autonomously.

In the analysis of developmental systems the relationships among the components can neither be deterministic nor uniform. What is of theoretical importance is the integration and disintegration of the components—the processes by which relationships among components become strengthened or weakened and change in their nature. Thus, in systems that are developing, there is a variety of types of relationships with different levels of strength.

USES OF SYSTEM CONCEPTS

The concept of a system can be used for several purposes. Two such will be used First, it can be used to express relationships among social "units" in order to define a social "object." Thus, the idea of a system delimits the interdependencies among some set of phenomena that constitute a social object, such as a city or country. The properties of such defined "objects" are the focus of this conceptual analysis. A second use of the concept of systems is as a grammar for a theory that expresses interdependencies among variables or properties. For defining social objects, the elements of the system would be class concepts of specific phenomena, such as economic institutions, or of a set of activities, such as production. For constructing theory, the elements (or vocabulary) of the system would be properties that vary (or variables).

The Definition of Development

The development of a system is its level of integrated diversity. The two properties comprising development are diversity and integration, each of which is defined. Development depends on the structure of interaction between these two general properties of systems. A system can have a high level of diversity and a low level of integration, or a high level of integration with little diversity. Since these two properties are not monotonically related, that is, as one increases, the other does not necessarily increase, it is necessary to look at their interaction in order to assess a system's development.

The Structure of Development: Diversity

Diversity is a structural property of a system derived from the distribution of its properties among its components. It is an aggregative structural relational property in that it is defined in terms of the relationships among properties of subsets with no implication of interdependence. Diversity is a property of both sets of objects and of the components of systems.[3]

VARIETY AND THE PROPERTIES OF A SYSTEM

For any set there is the total number of properties, based on counting the properties of the elements in the set.[4] Properties can be compared to determine which are identical and which are different. The variety of a set is the total number of different properties or the number of subsets of identities. Thus, for any set of properties there are: (1) the total number of properties; (2) the total number of different properties; (3) the total number of identical properties; and (4) subsets of identical properties. The latter equal the variety of the set.

Although a distinction has been made between properties that are identical (identities) and properties that are different (differences), any refinement of this binary language—how much or to what degree different—would strengthen the arguments that follow.

SIMILARITIES AND DIFFERENCES

The similarities and differences of a system or set are based on the distribution of the total number of properties into subsets or groups, which when they become properties of objects and are integrated, become components of a system.

Every subset of properties or system components thus can have properties that are both similar to or different from the properties of every other subset. Each property of any one subset that is shared by, is identical to, a property of any other subset is a similarity; each property of any one subset that is not shared by, is not identical to, any property of another subset is a difference. Similarities and differences are relational properties of subsets; their total number is an aggregative relational property of the total set of the subsets or of the system.

The maximum possible number of similarities for any system is the total possible number of identities across the subsets. Thus, for a set with 100 subsets and five properties in each subset, there would be nearly 25,000 possible identities, each identity across two or more subsets being a similarity:

$$\frac{N(n)}{2} \quad \frac{(n-1) \text{ or } 5(100)}{2} \quad (99) = 24,750$$

Differences are those properties of one subset not shared by other subsets. If no properties of any subset are shared by any other subset, again there would be the maximum possible number of differences, which would be equal to the maximum number of possible identities of properties across subsets. The total number of possible pairs of a system are precisely determinable, quantitative characteristics of a system.

DIVERSITY

Whereas both similarities and differences are based on property by property comparisons across components or subsets, diversity is based on comparisons of the total set of properties of each subset or component. Diversity is thus the extent to which the sets of properties of the components are not identical. It, too, is a quantitative concept.

It is possible, therefore, for systems to have both substantial similarities between their components and substantial diversity among their components. This is a crucial theoretical difference for the dynamics of development. It is a difference in levels among the components as a whole versus properties of the components. Whereas differences by themselves define cleavages or breaks in the structure of a social system, similarities and differences taken together are a structural condition for interdependence.

The proportion of the total properties of the components that are different defines the amount of diversity between any two components. Thus, if component one has properties A,B,C,D, and E and component two has properties D,E,F,G, and H, there are ten total properties, two similarities, and .60 diversity, that is the proportion of the possible to the actual differences. This calcula-

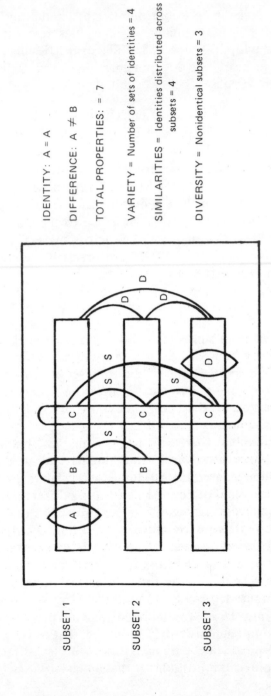

IDENTITY: A = A

DIFFERENCE: A ≠ B

TOTAL PROPERTIES: = 7

VARIETY = Number of sets of identities = 4

SIMILARITIES = Identities distributed across subsets = 4

DIVERSITY = Nonidentical subsets = 3

SUBSET 1

SUBSET 2

SUBSET 3

Figure 1: THE MEASUREMENT OF DIVERSITY

tion of diversity among two components can be extended to any number of components.

An alternative way to determine the diversity of a system is whether or not the total set of properties of a component is identical to or different from others—whether they are the same with respect to every property or are different, if there is only one property that is not shared. Diversity, thus, would be based on a "yes - no" decision for each pair of components—the total number of paired comparisons of components (N) (N-1)/2, where N is the number of components minus the number of observed identical components. Since whatever is concluded about this simpler formulation of diversity is also true of the more complex expression presented above, the simpler one will be used in this discussion.

The relationships between similarities, differences, and total number of properties can be interpreted in the following summary manner, indicating again how similarities and diversity are interdependent structural properties rather than independent of properties of sets or systems.

TYPES OF PROPERTIES:
OBJECT PROPERTIES AND PROPERTIES PROPER

A basic distinction is made between object properties and properties proper, a distinction which is fundamental to the dynamics of development change. The first, object properties, are material items to which one or more components are related, either by right or virtue of possession. Object properties are detachable from the component and transferable to other components. They occupy a unique place in time and space, and these locations have social implications. In part because they have a unique location in limited temporal and physical space, they are scarce, and consequently among the behaviors that they generate are competition and conflict. They also decay and are consumed.

Properties proper are nonmaterial properties of the component, such as skills, values, and knowledge. They cannot be detached from the component and transferable to other components. They not have a unique location in time and space. Their use and distribution do not detract from their value; rather, distribution enhances their value and strengthens their integration with all other properties of the component. Since they have no unique place in time or space, they do not involve competition and conflict.

This sharp analytical distinction, of course, is overdrawn; in reality, the value of ideas involves the capacity to have them take material form in order to facilitate the utilization of skills and knowledge. What is important to this theory is, however, the extent to which they differ in dominating and creating particular kinds of social relationships.

Once object properties are distributed two kinds of differences result among components. The first is a difference in quality—a component has an object property or it does not. These qualitative differences are the primary distinction used in the discussions of similarities and differences. A second difference is in the quantity of object properties. A component is different from another because it has two of the same kind of object properties, whereas the other has only one. These differences can be multiplied—three vs. one, four vs. one, etc. Two consequences of differences in quantity are used—the process of accumulating identities and the diminishing differences accruing from redundant identical properties. The former is the basis for producing new variety and thus diversity; the latter reduces the potential diversity that could be derived from distribution.

Properties proper are qualitative. There are, therefore, no redundant identities, and, hence, no component differences arise from quantitative differences in the same property. A component has a particular skill or it does not. It cannot have two skills of the same kind; it cannot know the same thing more than once. As properties proper, they have no unique location in time and space and, accordingly, they are not foci of competition and conflict unless access to them is restricted.

Three other types of properties will be used in this analysis. First, there are aggregative relational properties based on components sharing or not sharing properties with no implication for interdependence. Diversity is the primary aggregative relational property used in this analysis. Second, there are structural relationships among components that have implications for interdependence—equality, hierarchy, and cleavage. Changes in these relationships are a consequence of developmental change. Third, there are the properties of relationships, in particular the integration of components, which is independent of both aggregative relational properties and the nature of relationships. Integration is central to the concept of development.

As this is a general theoretical analysis, the kinds of object properties or properties proper that are relevant for particular kinds of systems are not specified. There are, however, some guidelines for determining which properties are relevant. Two general ones for defining relevant properties are the peculiarities of the system under examination and its level of development.

One major theoretical distinction among socially relevant properties is between those that primarily produce similarity and those that primarily produce diversity. Identifying socially relevant properties that affect social behavior can, to some extent, be derived from the theory and to some extent from knowledge about a specific social system. There are: (a) objectively observable properties, particularly object properties; (b) properties that are perceived to be (are responded to as if they are) similar or different, and (c) properties that have been found to explain behavior or that have some theoretical relevance for development.

The latter, for example, would be diversity–producing properties. These will tend to be new items object properties and properties proper, items just introduced in the system and being distributed. As newly introduced items continue to be distributed to the point that 50 percent of the components have them, their relevance for increasing diversity stops and shifts to increasing similarity, as will be discussed. Radios, for example, are developmentally relevant for many countries, contributing to the establishment of a system-level network of communications and serve as an important indicator for distinguishing between "developed and underdeveloped regions" or "modernized and traditional" sectors of the population. Their relevance as a source of increasing diversity for highly industrialized countries is negligible. Other items are now creating diversity.

Thus, the level of development as well as the past history of a system can suggest what kinds of properties are creating diversity within the system. It also should be clear that what is socially relevant and what is developmentally relevant are different. In highly industrialized societies radios may continue to be socially relevant but not developmentally important. Also, for some time a new item of variety may be developmentally relevant in terms of increasing diversity but unimportant in explaining more than a small amount of individual or group behavior.[5]

These guidelines speak for an approach of assessing which properties are developmentally relevant for particular systems rather than for systems in general. They do not solve the problem that one component, individual or organization, may differ from another by virtue of possessing a stamp collection and the other by virtue of owning a bank. Such distinctions require a weighting of each property or type of property in the context of particular systems.

The Structure of Developmental Behavior: Integration

Integration is the probability that a change in one component will lead to changes in other components. Integration is thus a characteristic of the relationships among the components of a system. Furthermore, some level of integration, some theoretical level, is definitionally necessary for a set to become a system, that is, to have interdependencies among components rather than aggregative relational properties among members of a set.

DIMENSIONS OF INTEGRATION

Integration is composed of three dimensions. They are dimensions proper in that they are all based on the same observations—the interdependencies among components—but expressed in a way that make relationships among them to some degree independent. Each dimension can be stated in the language of statistics.[6]

First, there is the strength of the interdependencies which is the probability that a change in one component will lead to a change in the other components. Strength of interdependence—"connectedness" for the system as a whole—refers to the average probability for all components across some stable number of time points. Strength neither refers to the extent to which the other components are linked nor to how many properties may change in the other components. Thus, a system with strong interdependencies could have two components, each having one property.

Second, there is the dimension of inclusiveness, which is the extent to which every component of the system has an equal probability of changing or being changed by other components without regard to the level or strength of that probability. Thus, a system could have little strength but be inclusive. There would be a small but equal probability of a change affecting all components. A distinction must be made between system components that are behaviorally a part of a system and physical units that are normatively but not behaviorally a part, like totally isolated individuals residing in a country. Such physical units are not theoretically a part of the system, and thus not components of the system. Only when there is some level of interdependence of the unit can it be said to be a component of the system, despite the normative reach of the system or its claims to inclusiveness.

The third dimension of integration is extensiveness, the proportion of all properties of the components that are affected by changes in other components. Thus a system can be highly integrated on the dimensions of strength and inclusiveness, but the system affects only a small proportion of all properties held by components. A system may be integrated economically, but not so politically.[7] To the extent that certain types of properties are not affected by the system is the extent to which the system is not integrated. What is important in extensiveness is the proportion of properties of the components rather than the total number of properties or their variety.

INTEGRATION

In a totally integrated system, the maximum level of integration would be one in which every property of every component would change with an equiprobability of 1.00 with any change in any component. A perfectly integrated system would be strictly closed and strictly determined. Any empirical social system, of course, has "slack," the difference between the maximum possible and the actual level of integration.

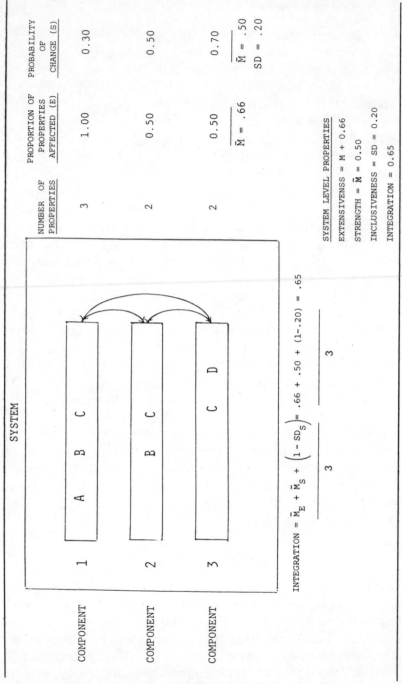

Figure 2: SCORING SYSTEM INTEGRATION

Integration is an equal weighting of these three dimensions. Such an equal weighting, of course, does not imply which dimensions are more or less important for the stability of particular systems at different levels of development. At low levels, the most important focus for the analysis of a system's development would be increasing its strength. For more highly developed systems, strength and inclusiveness might be high and the dimension of integration most rapidly increasing would be extensiveness, incorporating new areas of behavior into the system.

Integration as a concept composed of these equally weighted three dimensions is illustrated in Figure 2 for a hypothetical system of three components.

Although the concept of integration properly refers to a system and its components, it is possible to express how well each component is integrated with the system, and to compare its level of integration. Again, at different levels of development, different types of components will be more integrated than others. How well integrated a particular component is with the system depends on the probability of each of its properties being affected by changes in other components and the differences or variances in those probabilities for each property. Thus, the higher the mean probability and the less the variance, the higher the integration of the component with the system. For example, if a component has five properties and the probability of each being affected by changes in other components is A=.5, B=.4, C=.3, D=.2, and E=.1, the integration of the component would be the Mean Probability/ Standard Deviation or .3. Since components may be made up of other components, that is, subsystems, it is possible to speak of the integration of these subsystems in the same definitional language as that for analyzing the integration of all types of systems.

ELABORATION OF INTERDEPENDENCIES

The concept of integration as a quantitative property of systems does not refer to the nature of the relationships, whether they are reciprocal or hierarchical, whether there are few or many, whether they are temporary or durable. According to the definition of integration a system could have a dense network of relationships among its components and yet have a lower level of integration than a system with only one or two relationships. Social systems are, in fact, characterized by low levels of integration, at least in comparison to mechanical or biological systems.

With development, however, there is an elaboration of relationships, an increase in both the number and types of relationships. This elaboration is explained in part by the differentiation of levels of subsystems—the aggregation of components into groups and their deaggregation. In part, it is explained by the dynamic of integrating diversity, which changes the relationships among the components. The elaboration of types and the intensification of relationships are, however, independent of the level of integration alone. It results, rather, from the dynamics of developmental change, which involves changes in relationships.

Development: The Interaction Between Diversity and Integration

Integration and diversity are both independent and interdependent. Their interaction constitutes one of the two basic dynamics of developmental change and is the basis for assessing the level of development of a system. Increases in development involve a process by which the levels of integration and diversity are reconciled. An interpolation of both the values of integration and diversity at a given point in time defines the level of development of a system; an increase in development is based on increases both in diversity and integration.

Disintegration occurs if diversity increases but integration either remains constant or decreases. Stagnation occurs if integration continues to increase without an increase in diversity. The former will eventually lead to system collapse. The latter to slowly running down the system. If both integration and diversity decline, then there is developmental retrogression, but not necessarily disintegration and collapse or running down and stagnation. Because integration and diversity continue to be locked into their interactive pattern even when both are declining, it is possible for the system to reverse its course.

DEVELOPMENT, DEVELOPMENTAL PROCESSES, AND DEVELOPMENTAL CHANGE

Development is defined as the level of integrated diversity at any point in time. Developmental processes are the interaction of integration and diversity over several points in time such that the level of integrated diversity increases. The logical consequences of developmental process are developmental change and the transformation of the system. Developmental change is defined as a change in either the nature of the components of a system or in the relationships among them, or both.

For a given number of components and with an assumption of an upper limit on the number of properties that can be held by each component (to be elaborated in the following chapter), it is possible to determine the maximum level of diversity of any system. The definition of integration also specifies a maximum level. At those points in the developmental process where the maximums of both are approached (allowing for some system slack which is posited as being a universal characteristic of social systems because of the autonomous nature of both diversity and integration), the system can neither become more integrated nor more diverse. As the system approaches these upper limits, it either stagnates, or generates new components and relations. If the latter, then the system becomes transformed. It is unlikely, however, that these changes, outside of some historical events, would change all at once. In highly developed systems, for example, there are elements of the new type of system emerging, once the system begins to reach its upper limit of integration and diversity.

Development, then, is a quantitative concept, developmental process is an increase in this quantity, and developmental change, a qualitative concept. Development is, therefore, one part of social change—that which increases the level of integrated diversity of a system. Developmental change is another part of social change—changes in components and relationships that result from developmental processes. This means that if social change is defined literally, as changes in the values of properties of a social system or its components over time, development and developmental change may be only a small domain of the social change taking place.

DEVELOPMENT AND SIZE

The scale, or level of development of a system, is logically independent of its size. Size has two meanings: the number of physical
entities encompassed within some boundary definition and the
number of components of a system. Because development refers
to the diversity across components and the integrative linkages
among them, it is independent of size defined either as the number of physical units or components. Contemporary national
political systems, for example, vary from small size and large scale
to large size and small scale systems.

For systems at low levels of development there is a size-scale
limit, depending on the number of properties that can be possessed by any component and the number of components. This
size-scale limit is one factor contributing to the distribution of
properties among components within a system and thus to increasing development.[8] At a certain level of development, however, the
system can escape its size limitation and enter an exponential developmental stage. This occurs either by deaggregating components
or by the transfer of component properties to the system, both of
which are discussed in the following chapter. With deaggregation
the system increases its number of components and by transferring properties to the system, it frees the components to take on
or absorb additional items of variety. With low levels of diversity
and integration, for example, the major components of the system
are groups and collectivities with individuals submerged in them.
Individuals as autonomous components are not a characteristic of
small scale systems. With development, more groups differentiate,
stopping at the point where the individual becomes the primary
component of the system. In this sense, development creates system "size," but without any necessary actual increase in the number
of physical units in the system. Thus, in the assessment of development, per capita indicators are meaningless, unless it is known
that the individual is an actor or component in the system, something which this theory can in part explain.

Population increase is, of course, one means by which a system
can transform its existing variety into diversity, and, potentially,
into an increase in its level of development. But population increases will contribute to development only if a system is variety

rich and component poor. One alternative that can compensate for lack of diversity, is to open the system to variety and diversity outside of it, a factor that is exogeneous to this theory.

THE ASSESSMENT OF DEVELOPMENT: DIRECT AND INDIRECT

The concept of development defined as integrated diversity provides a basis for an exact assessment of the development of an empirical system. What is implied in the concept is a measurement system with a measurement language for ordering observations and combining them. It does not provide for measurement operations for specific systems that would specify observations. Such measurement operations have to be provided outside this or any theoretical framework.

Two kinds of measurement of development are presented below in order to explicate a measurement system for the concept of development. The first is direct measurement, where each component would be observed and compared with others. Such a measurement system would be feasible for small scale systems.[9] The second is indirect assessment, or making inferences about diversity and integration from some readily available indicators that have been assembled for different purposes. In indirect measurement, it is difficult to use a general inference rule so that every case of a higher score on the indicator would mean a higher level of integration or diversity. Indicator measurement contains error and among this error for the concept of development is that the indicators often do not indicate diversity independently from integration. Both types of measurement presented, however, further clarify the concept of development.

The definition of development points to measurement for the direct assessment of the development of any empirically defined social system. Direct assessment of diversity would involve: (1) selecting socially relevant properties, both object properties and properties proper; (2) comparing each property of each component with every other one; (3) identifying the similarity and differences among the properties of every component with those of every other one; and (4) computing the combination properties of every component to determine whether each set differs from every other set. These steps would provide a basic or direct measurement statement for the diversity and the amount of similarity of every system as well as yield an approximation of the total variety of the system, which at the very least includes every different property of the components.

In order to standardize diversity scores for cross-system comparisons, the proportion of total components that are identical or different as a proportion of total possible identical can be used. An example would be a system with 100 components with 20 that are different in their combination of selected properties. First, there is the total number of potential identical components, which for 100 components would be pairs of all components or 4,950. Second, there is the actual number of components that are identical, which is 80, for a total number of identical pairs of 3,160. Third, there is the difference between the potential identical components and those actually identical, which is in the example, 1,790. The proportion of those that are not identical to those that could be identical is .36, which would be the diversity score for this set expressed as a proportion.

Whereas, in the case of integration, there is a specific range of scores, varying from 0.00-1.00, the potential total diversity of a system is dependent on both the number of components and the number of properties. As the properties selected for assessing diversity would vary with the system under study and the number of properties that would be selected as relevant to diversity would increase with development, a measure of diversity for a total development score that is better suited to cross-system analysis is comparisons of increases and decreases or rates of increase and decrease rather than comparisons of actual scores. Comparisons of increases and decreases would discount the context of particular systems and compensate for the use of system-specific properties as developmentally relevant. An international standard of comparison would require knowing how much variety is possible on a global level, and then assessing a particular system's variety and diversity according to what proportion of the total global properties were manifest in the diversity of the components of a particular system.

For integration, it would be necessary to observe every component over some length of time in order to determine the probability that it would be affected by changes in other components.

This would require determining how many of the total properties of every individual component are affected by any change and the actual probability of any change for every component. The later observation would be the basis for computing the equiprobality (standard deviation). These two observations, and one derivation, are expressed in a statistical language which allows for their combination, as discussed above.

In indirect assessment, indicators of development should correlate with development scores derived from the basic measurement operations. The indicators that could be used for the assessment of particular social systems would be phenomenological manifestations of development as defined, and thus must be delimited by the historical context of that system.

One crude set of partially available indicators of diversity for contemporary countries is the simple categorization of the population into economic sectors—primary, secondary, tertiary, quartary. Since production has such generalized implications, the economic activities of the population in terms of the variety of skills required in each sector might be suitable for industrializing countries. An example of the use of these indicators would be an arbitary but monotonically increasing weighting of each of these sectors to reflect increasing levels of variety: "1" for primary; "2" for secondary; "3" for tertiary; and "4" for quartary. The proportion of the total population in each sector would be multiplied by these weights. If the population is 50 percent primary, 30 percent secondary, and 20 percent tertiary, a crude estimate of the diversity of the system would be the index number $1.7 = [(.5 \times 1) + (.3 \times 2) + (.2 \times 3) + (0 \times 4)]$. It would be possible, of course, to take into account differences within each of these sectors, and thus obtain more accurate estimates of diversity. Such estimates, again, could be used for cross-national comparisons and cross-time analyses.

This illustration of indirect assessment of diversity is based on national aggregates. Territorial units or regions within the country are a better aggregative base for less developed countries and sectors for more developed systems. Some indicators of individual level diversity might be required, particularly for highly developed systems. In this case, most available census data are too limited for more than crude estimates of total differences among the population; survey research, however, may provide more extensive individually based data on similarity and diversity.[10]

Indicator assessment of integration is more problematical than that of diversity. One approach to indicator measurement is correlations among properties of all components of sectors of components. If it were possible to obtain an approximate sample of correlations (correlations are used here as one expression of relationships), then these correlations could be used as indicators of interdependence, even if only at one point in time, although developmental processes require indicators of integration focused on changes over time.

First, the average correlations among properties in various sectors or regions could be used as an index of the strength of interdependence. If, for example, average correlations among these properties within sectors or regions were approximately .3, then .3 could be taken as the best estimate of strength. Second, there is the variability in the correlations among the sectors or the consistency of the relationships. An index of inclusiveness would be the variance in correlations across sectors or regions. For example, in one region of a country the correlation between economic status and political attitudes could be positive, in another negative, and in a third, nearly random. In this case, the index of inclusiveness for the country would be quite low, as the relationships are highly variable. Third, the same set of correlations could be used to estimate the extensiveness of integration. Again, if it can be assumed that the set of indicators is a sample of all indicators, then the proportion of those that are correlated (at some arbitrary level) to those that are not, could be used as an index of the extensiveness of integration. These three indices could be combined into an estimate of integration based on the three dimensions of integration.

This indicator approach to the assessment of integration puts the nature of empirical hypothesis testing in social research into a radically different context. Although most social research formulates hypotheses to focus on what is probably not random, this perspective on development and its assessment through indicators assumes that the level of development determines how much variability or variance there is in the system and how many nonrandom relationships exist. Furthermore, the relationships among indicators are viewed generally as a set rather than specifically in terms of one variable against another. Thus, whether and to what extent the assumptions of modern social science research are viable depends on the level of development of the system being studied.

STAGES OF DEVELOPMENT

Theories of development either explicitly or implicitly contain stages of development, suggesting "qualitative changes" that set apart one stage from another. Some imply that one stage is necessarily prior to another or that one type of system will necessarily be transformed into another. Stages are, however, often more a description than a logical consequence of a theory development. As was discussed in the introduction, this theory does not state that development is a historical necessity for any particular empirical system and, consequently, that one stage follows another. The theory provides for a transformation of systems—developmental change—that follows as a logical consequence of some conditions being present at a previous stage, when the system approaches its maximum limits of diversity and integration. If the maximum limits are reached, then for more development to occur, there must be a new "integrating" principle or a qualitatively different stage—a transformation of the system.[11] Such an interpretation does make a historical necessity out of a logical consequence by definition. This theory does not state whether a system will develop or whether it will follow a particular path of development. It does state that if a system is to develop it necessarily will have to be of a particular type and will necessarily have to become transformed.

NOTES

1. Macroqualitative changes embrace radical discontinuities, new stages, system transformation, and system disintegration.

2. Simply linking two elements also constitutes a change, bringing a system into being.

3. When a set "becomes" a system, all properties of that set, such as size, are properties of the system. The opposite is not true.

4. A set can be composed either of properties or objects, either defined (e.g., the set of all cities), or undefined (e.g., a set of "empty" logical terms).

5. This discussion does not address the distinction between "essential" and "marginal" changes, criteria for which have to be specified, but rather only that between developmental and nondevelopmental change. Also, a distinction can be made between those properties that are likely to be used to produce new properties that will increase diversity and those that will be used to maintain a distribution of properties through replacement. What particular properties are "investments" in development must be defined in terms of the context of the level of development and the history of development of a system.

6. Statistical concepts are used here for measurement. Such concepts are not suitable for analyzing developmental dynamics.

7. To the extent that there are sectors of behavior differentially integrated into the system with regard to extensiveness it is appropriate to speak of economic, political and social subsystems.

8. Redistribution by governmental action can, depending on the size-scale relationship, either reduce or increase the overall level of development.

9. Direct measurement of large scale systems would require large sustained research, such as has been given to measuring gross national product.

10. Education would be an appropriate substantive domain for indicators of individual diversity on properties proper.

11. New "integrating" principles are perhaps most readily seen in the explicit rules of political systems, such as slaves and freemen; group membership, and individual citizenships; private ownership, and social ownership, etc.

Chapter 2

THE DYNAMICS OF STRUCTURAL

DEVELOPMENT

The core of the structural dynamics of developmental change is that the greater the total number of properties available for distribution, the greater the variety of those properties; and the greater the number of properties distributed to each component, the greater the diversity of the total system. To the extent that this greater diversity is integrated, it will yield greater variety. The probability that diversity will become integrated increases to the extent that greater diversity is accompanied by greater similarity. And the more diversity there is, the more rapidly variety increases; and the more rapidly variety increases, the more rapidly diversity increases. An increase in one accelerates an increase in the other—if increases in diversity are accompanied by increases in similarity—and the integration of diversity increases.

Thus, the level of development predicts the rate of development. Predicting the level of development at any point in time requires knowing the level of development at a previous time, as well as the rate of development (which can be derived from knowing the level of development at that previous time).

One structural dynamic of development is the shift—back and forth—between the diversity of the components and the variety of the system. Furthermore, with such shifts there are fluctuations in the rate of development. Changes in the nature of these relationships are some of the qualitative changes that occur as a result of quantitative increases in aggregative diversity.

Structural Development: An Overview

Structure refers to the relational properties among the components and between the components and the system as a whole. Of the two types of structural properties of the components, relational properties and aggregative relational properties, the latter will be the focus of this discussion of structural change.

Relational properties proper, such as equality and hierarchy, will change as a result of changes in the aggregative relational properties. This view of the dynamics of structural change holds that changes in relational properties proper, such as those among individuals, are both a precondition and a consequence of aggregative structural change. Whereas aggregative structural change is always quantitative by definition, changes in the nature of relational properties are always qualitative, also by definition.[1]

What must be shown is that an existing number of components can take on a greater number of properties in such a way that both similarities and diversity can be increased at the same time. The law of aggregative diversity and inclusive similarity demonstrates that this is both a logical and empirical possibility. Nevertheless, there is a limit to the number of properties that can be held by any component. Aside from mechanisms to overcome this conflict between increasing system variety and its consequent diversity, such as increasing the population of components or preventing an increase in variety, there are two basic structural dynamics for continually increasing structural capacity for diversity. The first is to transfer an item (object properties and properties proper to the system), thereby transforming the item from a diversity-yielding property to a system similarity, providing additional system capacity for diversity. The second structural dynamic is the structural migration of properties from lower levels of aggregation, subsystems, to higher ones. The latter are able to absorb more variety, allowing again for additional variety to be taken on by components at lower levels. This is called the law of attractiveness of variety and is critical to the processes of integrating diversity, which is discussed in the following chapter.

The Law of Aggregative Diversity and Inclusive Similarity

The law of aggregative diversity and inclusive similarity, taken from the logic of probability, states that the greater the number of total properties of the system, the greater the variety of those properties, and the greater the number of properties of each component, the greater the probability that each component will be similar to others in an increasing number of specific ways and be different as a whole.

What is critical is the distinction between levels: the probability of any single property in any set of properties being similar to others and the probability of any two sets being identical in their totality. This distinction in levels means that as the total number of properties and their variety increase, and as the number of properties in each subset (the subset of properties possessed by a component) increases, the probability of similarities obtaining between the properties of pairs of components will increase linearly, and the probability of diversity or "uniqueness" of the total set of properties between pairs of components will increase exponentially.

In order to explicate this law and to place it in the context of integrated diversity, two things are necessary. First, it must be shown that the probability of any subset having properties that are similar to those of other subsets is a linear function of the number of properties in the set, the number of different properties in that set, and the total number of properties of each subset. Second, it must be demonstrated that the possible unique outcomes in terms of combinations of properties are exponential functions of the number of properties, the number of different properties, and the total number of properties of each subset. This is basic to the logic of structural development. It is the basis of exchange that takes place at certain levels of development. Unique components are possible, having several properties similar to others rather than only different properties.

What are the probabilities of a similarity among any two components of a system? It is a conjunction of the two probabilities of each having a specific property. Random sorting of properties into subsets will be assumed to be the equivalent of assigning or distributing properties to components of a system.[2] The probability of each component having property A depends on the number of A's in the set, the total number of non-A's in the set and the total number of properties in the set. For example, if there are 100 properties and there are 20 A's, 20 B's, 20 C's, 20 D's, and 20 E's (variety = 5), then the probability, when randomly assigning one property to the first component and randomly assigning another property to another, of a specified similarity in the two components is the product of the two probabilities (.2 X .2 = .04).[3] However, the probability of the first component containing an A is the sum of the probabilities of obtaining an A on each of several independent random assignments. Thus, if two properties were assigned to a component, the probability of at least one of them being an A would be .36,[4] and the probability that the first and the second component both possessed an A would be .36 X .36 = .13. The probability of both having an A increases exponentially with increases in the number of properties assigned to each.

The first part of the law of aggregative diversity and inclusive similarity can be generalized. First, there is the total number of properties N; second, the number of different properties, V_1, V_2 ... V_n; third, the number of properties of each component n_1, n_2 ... n_n. If an equal distribution of the number of different properties for each component is assumed (this linear result would also occur if there were an unequal number of different properties of each), then:

(1) For the probability that any one specified property of one component being similar to the same as, that of another would be:

$$P = \left(\frac{V}{N} \ X \ \frac{V}{N} \right)$$

or in the above example of

$$P = \frac{(20)}{100} \ X \ \frac{(20)}{100} = .04$$

(2) For the probability that any property of one component would be similar to that of another:

$$P = \left[\frac{V_1}{N} \cdot \frac{V_1}{N}\right] + \left[\frac{V_2}{N} \cdot \frac{V_2}{N}\right] + \ldots \left[\frac{V_n}{N} \cdot \frac{V_n}{N}\right]$$

or $\left(\frac{V_1}{N}\right)^n + \left(\frac{V_2}{N}\right)^n + \ldots \left(\frac{V_n}{N}\right)^n$

where the exponent is the number of components to which properties have been assigned, or in the above example of two components and two properties, the probability of at least one A in each component is $2(.2)^2 + 2(.2)^2 = .16$.

The variety or number of different properties reduces the probability of similarities in that the probability of any two specific independent outcomes being alike is reduced; the total number of properties increases the probability of any two outcomes being alike, and the total number of properties of each component increases the probability of a similar property in each component, even if the number of those properties is unequal across components. Thus, to increase the similarity in a system, the total variety can be reduced, the total number of properties can be increased, or the total number of properties of each component can be increased.

Again, the law of aggregative diversity states that the greater the number of total properties, the greater the variety of those properties, and the greater the number of properties of any component, the less the probability that the configuration of properties of components will be identical, or conversely, the greater the probability that the sets of properties of components will be unique or diverse. Whereas for similarity the problem is to assess the probability that among any two components or all components one or two or more specific properties will be similar, the problem for diversity is to assess the probability that in any set of component properties the combinatorial outcomes will be unique. If there are three properties, A, B, and C, the combinatorial unique possibilities are 2^n in the case of three properties, 8 unique sets, including the set with no properties. In order to realize this diversity of outcome, it is necessary, of course, to have several A's, several B's, etc. Once these different properties are randomly assigned, then the probability of obtaining a unique set is a function of the total number of properties, the total number of different properties, and the total number of properties of each component. This relationship is, however, exponential.

A simultaneous increase in both the probability of similarity and the probability of diversity with increases in the number of properties of the components, the number of properties of the system, and the number of different properties, can obtain only if there are many of each or most properties. It is necessary, therefore, to allow for diversity to come about as a result of various frequencies of the same property. An individual who has one apartment is similar to someone who has one apartment, but both similar to and different from someone who has two apartments. For example, instead of the properties, A, B, and C, the properties A, A, B can be taken. This means that a component can have two A's rather than one as a possible combinatorial outcome. By allowing for combinations of identical properties, the potential diversity (unique outcomes) is reduced by two, but the potential similarities are increased substantially. By allowing for more than one identical item to be assigned to a component the potential diversity is traded off for similarity.

The logic of multiple similarity and differences producing linear increases in the probability of similarity and exponential increases in the probability of diversity at different levels of development will be explicated with the elaboration of the following outcomes.

The Distribution of Properties

The foregoing was a discussion of combinatorial possibilities, outcomes in terms of properties of similarity and difference and differences and diversity.[5] The basic issue for structural change is how these properties are distributed among components and the consequences of such distributions for development.

The general proposition on which the theoretical relevance of the distribution is based is that the greater the similarities and the diversity of components of a system, the greater the probability that they will interact and become interdependent.[6] For any component to be a member of the system it must be interdependent in at least one way. This means, first, that the structural requisite for any interdependence is at least one shared characteristic with at least one other component.[7]

Second, for any component to interact, rather than react, it must be different in at least one way from at least one other component. Without such a difference there would be no distinction between interaction and simple similarity of response. Thus the minimal aggregative relational structural characteristic of any component to be a member of a system is at least one similarity and one difference with at least one other component, not necessarily the same other component.

A hypothetical example of the distributions of various properties will illustrate the difference between maximizing similarity, maximizing diversity, and maximizing both diversity and similarity, the structural definitional characteristic of development. Take a set of 100 components, two types of properties, A and B (variety = 2), and 75 properties of A and 25 of B (total number of properties = 100). To maximize similarity, the total number of possible similarities, would require an equal distribution of properties. In this example, each component would have one. The total number of similarities would be $75(75-1)/2 + 25(25-1)/2$, for a total of 3,075. Such a distribution would mean structural cleavage—by definition differences produce cleavages if they are not complemented by similarities. In effect there would be two separate "systems"— those "components" with A and those with B. To maximize diversity would require the allocation of unique sets of A and B: one of A and one of B; one of A and two of B; two of A and one of B, etc. A distribution in which the total number of properties would be allocated to maximize diversity would exhaust the number of properties and exclude some components from having any properties.

To maximize the number of components that would be both similar and diverse (i.e., that would have at least one property in common and be different with respect to their combination to others) would require allocating at least one A. The components that would be given the remaining properties would share at least one, but differ in the combination of properties. Maximizing diversity, requiring allocating only one property to some, would yield structural cleavages since some components would not share a property. Maximizing both similarities and diversity would be inclusive of all components that had any one property.

The law of aggregative diversity states the logical possibility of diversity. Diversity is an exponential function. Similarity is a linear function of the number of properties of the system and of the components. Diversity is an exponential function of variety and the total number of properties of both the system and the components. The allocation of properties and their variety to a large extent determines how this law is realized in empirical systems; for it is the actual distribution of properties among existing components that is the basis for assessing the diversity and similarity of a system. Empirical systems can be characterized by whether they tend to maximize similarity, or diversity, or both similarity and diversity.

One common distribution of properties in social systems is a pyramidial or hierarchical distribution, such that almost every component has property A, a smaller number property B, and still fewer property C, etc. This would be an ordered distribution of properties and is at the core of any structure of social stratification. Such an ordering would tend to maximize existing properties and variety for integrating a social system. In contrast, an "abundant" system would be one in which every component had everything. Abundance would produce equality. Under conditions of scarcity, the "perfectly hierarchical" structure would maximize inclusiveness or would be totally inclusive, while it would, at the same time, maximize diversity; the "perfectly egalitarian" society would be totally inclusive, diminishing diversity.[8] Development dynamics feed upon an inclusive system that maximizes both diversity and similarity.

The Law of Diminishing Diversity

The total number of properties of a given variety exponentially contributes to system diversity up to a point where additional properties of that variety diminish the rate of increase in the system's diversity. This is the law of diminishing diversity; a corollary concerning the contribution to diversity of multiple properties of the same variety will be discussed.

If there are three properties, A, B, C, then, as has been shown, the combinatorial possibilities for diversity are unique combinations of A, B, C. The unique possible outcomes would begin to diminish at the point where the total number of properties of A exceeded (assuming they are randomly distributed) .5 of the total possible unique outcomes. Thus, for three properties, A, B, C, there are eight possible outcomes (2^n). Four of each property are required to realize these unique combinations in terms of components. However, once the number of A's exceeds one half of the total number of unique possible outcomes, the contribution of additional A's to the diversity of system diminishes. This, of course, is the familiar point that what is unusual is distinctive and what is ordinary is not. As the diversity diminishes with the multiplication of properties, similarity continues to increase. When the total amount of properties of a given variety exceeds .5 of the total possible unique combinations, the additional properties contribute more to increasing similarities than to diversity.

Diversity also occurs by components having two or more of the same properties. It is possible, for example, for a component to be unique if it had two automobiles, whereas all others had none or one. Giving components more than one property of a particular variety, however, does not increase the similarities of the system, as one property of a given kind provides the basis of similarity in a binary fashion.

A corollary to the law of diminishing diversity follows from a component having multiple identical object properties. The contribution to diversity of redundant identities held by any component is a negative log function of their number in that such items are "withheld" from other components which if they possessed them would increase the probability of their being different, thus adding to the diversity of the system.

The Law of Attractiveness of Variety

The law of attractiveness of variety states that components will tend to interact more with those components with nearly equal, equal, or greater variety and less with those with less variety. The exception is those units with identical variety. Furthermore, there will be a slightly stronger predisposition of those components with slightly less variety to interact with those with slightly more variety.

This law will be used to explain the drift of variety upwards to higher levels of aggregation in the system, which is one of the characteristics of the dynamics of integrating diversity to be discussed in the following chapter.

Whether this is a "law" as the term has been used or an assumption is questionable, as is also the case with the law or assumption of upper limits below. As an assumption, it could be expressed as some gravitational function, where the greater the variety of components, the more likely they will be to interact, and indeed, exchange variety for still greater variety. As an assumption, it could be defended with empirical evidence that the most developed countries exchange their complementary variety in technology, or that the more educated individuals interact more with those with similar levels but different types of education. As a law it could be established by introducing an assumption which is largely exogeneous to this systemic theoretical context: the preference of components and individuals to increase their variety. If it were true that in general variety is preferred or valued, then the systemic law of attractiveness of variety could be properly derived as an aggregate consequence of this component preference. This "preference" is the major link between the subjective state of individuals, or components, and the system in this theory. It is also used to explain exchanges among components. Either as a law or an assumption it is developmentally relevant only when the basic needs of individuals as components have been met.

The consequence of such a preference of a component to increase its variety would be an increase in its social space. It can, from the law of inclusive similarity and aggregative diversity, interact with a large number of components, including those with less variety, as well as increase its probability of interacting with components with more variety. Increased social space would be the social value of variety in contrast to its psychological desiderata.[9]

The Assumption of Upper Limits

With increases in both variety and the total number of each kind of variety, there will be increasing diversity of the system, one of the definitional elements of development. In order for this to be true, that is for diversity to increase as a consequence of variety and the total properties of a system, a dynamic of distribution is required. Distribution of variety and the properties derives from an upper limit to the variety that any component can hold.[10] The assumption of upper limits states that there is a maximum amount of variety that any component can hold. Because it is an assumption rather than a theoretical statement, a few arguments of justification will be presented.

For individuals, such an assumption is both theoretically and empirically sound. One way of expressing this upper limit for individuals is in the language of cognitive dissonance. It states that for individuals there is a limited number of types or cognitive components that can be comfortably or consistently retained at the same time. Two implications of this are that the total set of properties of any individual in some ways must be related by some principles of "consistency," and that at some point increasing the range of variety will entail psychic costs that will begin to outweigh the desirability of having additional variety. Using common sense, an individual who has multiple roles pays a price for those roles unless they are mutually reinforcing. Furthermore, although there are differences in ability to hold various amounts and kinds of variety, these differences will not be substantial. This assumption of upper limits is critical to understanding why with development there is a shift away from lower level components to higher level ones, as well as a shift away from organizations to individuals as dominant system components. With development there will be a tendency to distribute the total number of properties equally among components, although not necessarily specific kinds of properties.

For organizations the upper limit on variety is consonant with certain ideas of information theory. One such idea is that the greater the number of possible outcomes or states of the system, the greater the system entropy, and thus the greater the amount of information required to communicate. Organizations performing multiple tasks are inefficient to the extent that the tasks are numerous and independent, not mutually reinforcing, thus, reducing variety increases efficiency. The point at which the costs of information begin to exceed the advantages of variety would be the upper limit of variety for the organization. Empirically, of course, this upper limit varies with the type of organization, the nature of competition, and other forces.[11]

As development continues there will be more and more "vertical integration" of organizations. The logic of integrating diversity operates for organizations as well as social systems. Larger scale organizations are generally more productive than smaller scale ones, as will be discussed in Chapter 4.

Variety is the cornerstone of the collective rationale of social systems. There are no upper limits on diversity of developing systems in the long run. In the short run, there are upper limits, which can be overcome by further development or incorporation into systems of greater diversity.

Transfer of Variety to the System

In a strict statistical, aggregative sense, if there is no diversity among the components of a system, if, that is, the variety of every component equals the variety of the system, there are only system properties.

Items of diversity can be aggregatively transformed into a system property. This aggregative transformation of an item of diversity into a system property begins at the point of diminishing diversity discussed above. The process is completed when every component has that property, such as universal literacy. What was initially an item of producing diversity was transformed into an aggregative similarity.

Transforming an item from a primarily diversity producing one into a primarily similarity producing one vastly increases the total amount of similarities in the system. Every component shares that property with every other. Such a process does not, however, free the components to acquire additional diversity. Although additional numbers of the same kinds of properties contribute to the diversity or similarity of the system, they do not contribute to the total variety of the components, pushing the components to their upper limit of variety.

A process that is more fundamental to development in transforming variety into diversity and then similarity is the actual transfer of the property to the system. The property is available to all components from the system and, thus, need not be a property of the component. Such a transfer frees the components to acquire additional items of variety. This is particularly important in national economic development in meeting the basic needs of individuals. Drawing water is an item of similarity. When it is transferred to the system, as a water supply, the individual is freed from concern. Items of diversity and similarity of organizations can also be transferred to the system, such as when guaranteeing credit becomes a function of the government rather than of the organizations themselves.[12]

Again, because of upper limits and the constraints of size, a social system would eventually reach the point of its total potential diversity and would, therefore, cease to continue on its course of developmental change. One critical way of breaking out of the upper limits of diversity of the system is by transferring the property to the system.

Aggregation and Deaggregation

Systems with exponentially increasing diversity and a limit to the number of components that can absorb the potential diversity available from the number and variety of properties can increase their components, and, thus, their capacity to acquire more diversity by deaggregating their components. Ultimately, this means individuals rather than groups or institutions becoming the primary system component. The phenomenological manifestations of these decisive shifts, already underway in countries of large scale, are among the important qualitative differences emanating from quantitative increases in development.

With some level of diversity there is differentiation of the population and with some differentiation a growth in the number of groups and institutions. In most countries today groups and institutions are the dominant system components. With increasing diversity or potential for it, the institutions become too few in number to contain the actual diversity. In political participation, for example, a few political parties cannot represent or reflect the diversity of their members or of all people.

At the same time that certain units are deaggregating, others at higher levels of organized complexity are forming; either by taking variety from components with less variety or actually absorbing them. This is the consequence of the law of attractiveness of variety.

An additional reason for the breakup of social units into individuals is increasing individual variety. Thus, as individuals acquire more variety their association with social units becomes less rewarding, simply because the individuals' variety cannot be reflected in the modal positions of the social unit or aggregate. Thus, just as the system disperses variety into diversity by shifting downward to the individual as a social unit, so the individual, when he acquires more variety, pulls away from particular social units within the system and moves to levels of the system that have more complexity.[13] In effect, there is the rapid multiplication of the number of social units or components of the system, e.g., by decomposing composites into individuals.[14]

The consequence of the duality of this process is the breakup of intermediate social subunits and the emergence of levels of both greater complexity and similarity. Three general laws are at work. First, there is the law of requisite variety, which states that more encompassing systems must have empirically and definitionally more variety than any of their subunits.[15] It implies that if the system does not have greater variety than any of the subunits, then either the subunit will "leave" the system or else the system will collapse because of lack of control. Second, there is the proposition (derived from the law of inclusive similarity and aggregative diversity) that units with greater variety will also be more similar to those units of greater variety, not only because they share the general property of complexity, but also because of the greater probability that they share many specific properties. Thus, the larger the number of properties of a component, the greater the probability that they will share specific properties and be unique in their combination. What is true for aggregative properties of the system in general is also true for any subsets, here levels, of components. The third law that is operative, which has been previously discussed, is that of the attractiveness of variety.

Upper Limits, Equality, and Openness

All empirical social systems are loose rather than tight, that is, they never reach the full limits of their potential diversity. As development proceeds, there are alternative ways in which systems can continually expand their potential for diversity, thereby circumventing their upper limits.

The general systemic response to upper limits for closed systems is to distribute properties in such a way that more diversity is possible. When, with the distribution of properties, some proportion of the components begin to approach their upper limit of variety more actual diversity can be obtained by increasing the number of properties of those components that have not yet reached their upper limit. In the dynamics of developmental change, there is an equalizing tendency that becomes especially strong when the total potential for diversity is rising exponentially.[16]

A second type of system response to upper limits, which is outside of this discussion of closed systems, is to increase the number of components, thus increasing the degree of freedom for system diversity. This can be done either by natural increases in the population of the components or by actually importing components. The variety and the number of properties, for example, determine the question of whether population increases accelerate conventional economic growth or detract from it. If diversity is increasing exponentially and the equal distribution of properties does not keep pace with this growth, then population growth may be a positive factor in development; if the increase of the components, natural or otherwise, is faster than the increase in the number and variety of the system's properties, then increases in the number of components is a negative factor for economic growth. In the latter case, any distribution of properties would lead to a less inclusive distribution, not only decreasing developmental change, if any, but also increasing the number of component differences and thus cleavages. An increasing number of components will not have the minimum number of properties necessary for inclusion. Whether or not population increases are a factor in developmental change depends, in short, on exponential growth in the potential for diversity.

A third way in which systems can actualize their potential for diversity is by opening the system to others. What this simply amounts to is the addition of the variety of other systems or exporting variety to other systems. The development of the system is enhanced by integrating itself with the diversity of other systems.[17]

Additional Dimensions of Component Variety and System Diversity

Two kinds of variety at the component level have been discussed: (1) whether or not a property is present and (2) how many properties of a given variety are present. The discussion of similarities has been restricted to simply having or not having a property. Variety, however, is much more sensitive than simply having or not having a property. Small differences are often the basis for interaction. Furthermore, as development proceeds, smaller and smaller differences, or dimensions, of variety will become more decisive for interaction.

Two other dimensions of variety could be added. One is the dominance or the "rankings" that can be assigned to the properties of any component. For individuals this is obvious. A person may be both a citizen and an engineer, but subjectively attach more importance to engineering or objectively allocate more time to engineering than citizenship. Any number of rankings could be introduced to order the variety of any component and could be used as a basis in determining system diversity.

A second dimension of variety is the sequencing or timing of the acquisition of the property. Thus, in addition to the simple combinations of properties, the properties could also be ordered according to when they were acquired. The history of the component could thus be taken into account in determining the total diversity of the system.

Either of these two dimensions of variety would involve permutations, rather than combinations. They are presented here simply to indicate that the potential for diversity for most social systems is in fact a much more exponentially accelerating function than has been presented in the context of combinations. The important theoretical point, however, is the exponential increase in the possibilities for diversity with increases in variety. This point is sharpened if any kind of ordering of the properties were considered.

NOTES

1. As can be seen in the nineteenth and twentieth centuries, changes in relational properties within countries, such as those between landholders and land tenants, lead to aggregative structural changes, which in turn affect other relationships. Such changes, often introduced by purposeful political action, may increase the potential of the system for more diversity, but do not necessarily mean an increase in development—increases in both the diversity and integration of that diversity.

2. Random distributions are assumed for this discussion. Weaker assumptions, such as some randomness, should be sufficiently strong to support the arguments.

3. No adjustments are made for replacement in this discussion.

4. The probability of two non-A's is .8 X .8 = .64; of A and not A, .2 X .8 = .16; of not A and A, .8 X .2 = .16; and of A and A, .2 X .2 = .04. Thus, the probability of one A is .16 ⊢ .16 ⊢ .04 = .36.

5. This law amends the classical dichotomy of Durkheim between integration based on the mechanical solidarity of similarities and that based on functional interdependence or differences. The structural logic of development is that both similarities and diversity are the basis for integration.

6. One problem, in strategies for development, is the issue of whether to produce a large number of apartments or to allocate resources to the production of a variety of consumer goods. That strategic question must be as answered in terms of what increases integrated diversity or development.

7. For social systems a minimal shared characteristic would be a language of communications.

8. This structural logic in part explains the observed macrohistorical relationships between economic growth and increasing equality and economic stagnation and freezing economic inequalities. What it might add to such an explanation is the condition of the level of integration of a society. Thus, if a system has no economic growth, it may increase equality by reducing its level of integration. Of course, governmental intervention can redistribute, but at the price of some coercion to compensate for the disintegrating effects of redistribution.

9. This law is a weakly supported but necessary ingredient of this theory. It is probably generally empirically true. It is considered with other kinds of theoretical analyses, and it is consonant with this theory.

10. Both systems and components have variety. Components may have identical or different properties; only sets or systems have similarities and diversity. Complexity is a property of organized variety. Thus, both properties and components can be characterized as more or less complex. The complexity of properties is derived from the organization of variety that went into creating them through the processes either of combination or fusion. The complexity of components is based on how much variety they have and how well it is organized.

11. There is a process of losing efficiency by increasing variety, and of decreasing risk by increasing variety. Decreasing risk may be a more powerful incentive than the losses accruing from increasing variety, beyond a certain point. This "incentive" may

explain continued growth of certain economic organizations, despite losses in classical indicators of efficiency.

12. Developmental properties that are extensively similar are among the first to be transferred to the system, freeing a large number of components to acquire additional items of variety. At the individual level these involve water, sewerage, safety, etc., and are key initial developmental stimulants. Later these transfers involve power supply, housing, and transportation. This is discussed in later chapters as the process of socialization. Of course, in present circumstances the problem is insufficient numbers of properties for them to be integrated.

13. "Moving to" can include physically moving, changing interaction space, or expanding cognitive space. The latter two are characteristic of "cosmopolitans."

14. This process of aggregation and deaggregation is discussed again in the following chapter to explain the process of integrating diversity.

15. This law is attributed to W. Ross Ashby and plays an important part in the analysis of formal organizations.

16. Again, this does not, however, mean a distribution of identical properties.

17. Component population growth and exporting or importing variety are exogenous to this closed system theoretical approach. Empirically it is clear that some industrialized countries, particularly smaller ones, at some points need to import labor or involve themselves in an international division of labor. The problem with the economic development of less industrialized countries is that they are component "rich" and property "poor."

Chapter 3

THE DYNAMICS OF

DEVELOPMENTAL CHANGE

Developmental change is change in relationships among components and in the nature of the components that results from
development and results in a higher level of integrated diversity
of the system. These are changes in quality and thus transform
the social system.

The two central theoretical questions are: why does diversity
become integrated and why do the components of the system
change? Both can be addressed in the context of the dynamics
of developmental change in a closed system. They are related in
that the integration of diversity requires a change in the nature of
the components and the integration of diversity results in changes
in components. The first involves a conflictive interaction between
variety and integration, the second, shifts in variety across levels
within the system. The first is a dynamic across time, a consequence of two general system properties interacting across time;
the second is a dynamic across levels within the system, a consequence of the relationship between components with higher levels
of variety and organization of that variety and components with
less variety.

The Dynamics of Development
as a Process: An Overview

The dynamics of development over time can be described as a general process. In the integration of diversity the primary focus is on properties and the variety of those properties. The primary characteristic of this process is that variety reduces integration, and the integration of variety produces new variety. The following behavior over time describes this process: (1) variety is introduced into a system at a discrete point in time; (2) as that variety is distributed, it increases the system's diversity;[1] (3) increases in diversity reduce the level of integration of the system; (4) in response to diversity, integration occurs slowly over continuous time; (5) variety then is shifted, or moved, to components in the system with higher levels of organized variety; (6) those components, by taking on and absorbing the new variety, slow down the distribution of variety and the rate of increase in diversity; and (7) as this variety is absorbed and integrated, the probability of producing a new item of variety is increased. Once a new item of variety is produced, the process, described here for a single property, is reiterated.

For changes in the nature of the components, the primary focus is on the distribution of variety or diversity. Since variety is distributed unequally both in kind and quantity, there are components in the system with more or less variety and the organization of their variety or complexity. These components or levels attract those with slightly less variety. This attraction leads to transfers of properties to levels with greater variety and the incorporation of components at lower levels into those at higher levels, leaving some components at lower levels with less variety, but free to take on additional variety. Thus, there is differentiation among levels within the system, both through the incorporation of variety into higher levels and the deaggregation of components at lower levels. This process continues to a point where there are only components at the highest level of organized variety, the near equivalent of the system itself, on the one hand, and the components that cannot be further deaggregated, individuals, on the other. Intermediate levels of components within the system are absorbed by the system as a whole or by individuals behaving as components.

Although these processes have been presented as happening across time for a few components and a few items of variety, any empirical system of some complexity is a mosaic of levels, new variety, and transfers of properties—a mixture continually changing over time. Social systems, however, can be generally characterized as dominated by phases either of integrating variety or of reducing integration by taking on more variety. Social systems can also be characterized as dominated by certain levels of integration, centralizing certain activities in higher levels of organization, disassociating small groups and individuals from broader organizational and institutional ties, or, indeed, establishing the social basis of incorporating small groups and individuals into broader social, economic, and political frameworks, such as national associations, trade unions, or political parties. Such are the consequences of the dynamics of integrating diversity and of shifting levels of components within the system, the two basic dynamics of developmental change.

THE INTEGRATION OF DIVERSITY

In order to show why diversity becomes integrated and at higher levels, it is necessary to show: (1) why integration produces variety; (2) why variety reduces integration; (3) why reductions in integration do not generally, or most of the time, fall below some previous level; and (4) why increases of variety and diversity do not exceed the level of integration beyond a limit where it can be integrated. In addition, it is necessary to show why the rate of development increases as a function of the level of development. Such exponential increases are the basis of transforming one kind of system into another.

The dynamics of integrating diversity apply to those systems dominated by components with both similarity and differences. Developmental dynamics are engaged when social systems move away from dominance by similarities to differences and similarities. The conflictive consequence of these dynamics ceases when the system reaches high levels of integrated diversity and is dominated by components that are substantially different. Rapid and fundamental changes at this point in the quality of relationships constitute continuous developmental change.

INTEGRATION AND DIVERSITY: SYSTEMIC CONFLICT

Integration and diversity are in dynamic conflict which is zero sum at any one point in time and positive sum in the longer run. This conflict drives the system to higher levels of development and to developmental change.

The primary source of conflict derives from the behavior of variety and integration. Variety enters, is produced by, the system at one point in time, in instantaneous time. It appears in at least one component. The distribution of this variety yields diversity at an exponential rate, leveling off when 50 percent of the components have that variety. This exponential rate of increasing diversity, even from a limited distribution of variety, reduces the level of integration.

Integration takes place in continuous, linear time. Although as the level of development increases, the rate of this change increases, it remains linear in form. Decreases in integration, following from increases in diversity, however, are exponential, but slower than increases in diversity. These two different time functions explain the conflict between integration and diversity.[2]

Diversity reduces integration for the following reasons. First, the degree of integration of a component with the system is a positive function of the degree to which its variety is organized. The organization of this variety by the components takes some time. Thus, new variety reduces the degree of integration of particular components in the system and, thus, also the level of integration of the system itself. Second, any new variety taken on by a component at any point in time increases its total number of properties, and thus increases the base for the dimension of extensiveness of integration. One more property has been added, or a new property has been exchanged for an old; the new property must be linked to the system. Third, new variety alters existing relationships among components. In order to link the new property to other components, time is required for search and for establishing additional linkages.

Integration takes place in linear time for several reasons. First, when a new item is taken on, the component changes the diversity of the system. This change can be said to be instantaneous at that point. The linkages of components to others, however, are multiple and indirect through other components. Insofar as integration among components tends to take place one at a time, the strengthening of linkages will take linear time, which will be a function of the number of direct and indirect linkages. As those linkages, however, are elaborated and indirect, a few interactions spill over across several other components. Thus the rate of integration increases with the number of elaborated or indirect linkages, which is a function of the level of development of the system. As the level of the system's development increases, the rate of increase in integrating new diversity also increases.

Second, the organization of variety within the component requires time. The new item must be incorporated and then related to its existing properties. Once so related, it then becomes an integral part of the component, leading to spill-over effects such that any change in one property of the component will lead to changes in its others.

The organization of variety at the component level resulting in part from the integration of diversity at the system level increases the probability of that component producing a new item of variety. Not only is this a matter of the organization of variety at the component level, but also how well the system is integrated. If the system is highly integrated, then the probability that any component will obtain new properties conducive to producing new variety will be increased.

The production of new variety at any point in time by a component, and hence the possibility of new variety entering the system, reduces the level of integration, and the dynamic is reiterated. As the level of variety and diversity of the system increases, the probability of more variety being produced increases. Thus the level of variety and diversity, and the level at which they are integrated, contribute to one of the fundamental derived features of developing systems—as their level of development increases, their rate of development increases. This is only one of several factors that in combination contribute to an exponential rate development.

TECHNOLOGY AND DEVELOPMENT: A RESTATEMENT AND AN ASSUMPTION

Technology and technological change are parts of development and developmental change. Indeed, without technological change, there would be no development. It is necessary to explain why technology changes and why it changes social relationships. The concept of technology is often used to refer to the nature of the thing rather than its use. Two types of technology, one as a factor derived from development and the other as an empirical assumption, are related to increases in variety and the integration of diversity.

The first, "Technology I," is the creation of a new item of variety from existing items. Technological change thus defined is a social process that acquires a specific form at a point in time. It is the exact equivalent of creating a new item of variety. There are two types of this technology. First, there are combinations of object properties, labelled inventions. Such combinations are aggregations of existing object properties; they also can be de-aggregated. The rules by which they are aggregated are known. The second are the fusions of properties proper labelled innovations. The creation of a new idea or skill does not occur by combining properties proper but by fusing them in such a way that a new idea or skill emerges that is not a mere aggregation of the existing ones. Examples of the former are well known inventions, such as combining an engine with a cart, and of the latter, creating new areas of knowledge, such as microbiology. Increases in Technology I increase the probability that still more new items will be created. These new items can be compared with existing items, and some of them will be selected and combined into new inventions and innovations.

The higher the system's integration and the greater the variety of a system, the higher the probability that there will be new variety; and the greater the proportion of new technology to old, the greater the probability of creating still more variety. These statements strengthen the arguments made in the previous chapter; not only does diversity increase exponentially, but variety stimulates new variety, which feeds on existing variety to create still more variety.

The relationship between the amount of variety of the system and the probability of new variety being created can be expressed in terms of decreasing intervals of time required to create new variety. Thus the higher the level of diversity and variety, the shorter the period of time in which new variety will be created. This will accelerate the processes of increasing diversity and of faster integrative responses. Technology accelerates the rate of new technology, and it contributes to the general developmental process that the higher the level of development, the higher the rate of development.

The second type of technology, "Technology II," is an assumption rather than a description or a relabelling of some aspects of the developmental process. It is an assumption based on Technology I, and in part, it explains the increasing rate of integration. New items of variety, Technology I, are created, each having the potential of becoming either combined or fused with other properties. A certain proportion of those new items will facilitate interactions among the components. This is some proportion of Technology I, and as Technology I increases exponentially with the level of diversity and its integration in the system, Technology II should also follow an exponential curve. The consequence is to reduce the time-cost-distance barriers to interactions among components. Examples are transportation and communication.

Technology II, the proportion of Technology I that has the result of reducing time-cost-distance restraints, reduces the time taken for new variety to become integrated. It will be treated, as one of the contributing factors to increases in the rate of integrating diversity.[3]

INTEGRATIVE RESPONSES TO INCREASES IN VARIETY

The time functions of variety being translated into diversity as well as the increased probability of new variety obtaining from increases in variety means that the developmental dynamics result in unstable developmental processes. The time response of integration alone, taking place in a linear fashion could lead to system collapse. Variety and diversity would simply overtake and overrun the processes of integrating diversity.[4]

The theory does state, however, that there is a basic integrative response to new variety which initially reduces integration to reduce diversity. Without this response, the "natural" time required for integrating diversity would mean that eventually all developing systems would collapse from an accelerating rate of diversity.

The major integrative response to new variety is to reduce diversity by shifting variety to certain components and levels within the system that have greater capacity to absorb it. What this gains is time for integration at the expense of diversity. If new variety enters a system at some point in the system and begins to be distributed, generating diversity, that variety can be held or absorbed rather than distributed by certain components better than others (those components with greater amounts of variety and greater organization of their variety).

There are two reasons that levels of greater organized variety can absorb more variety than levels with less. First, any new item of variety in a large field of variety will be less "disturbing," that is, it is unlikely to deviate substantially from what the component already has. The disorganization introduced by any new item of variety is a function of the total amount of variety already possessed. Second, any component or level of components with a higher degree of organization of variety or integration of diversity will be disturbed proportionally less by any additional new item. The greater the number of linkages among the items within a component or components constituting a level, the less any new item will alter those linkages.

Items continually shift their places within a system. The law of the attractiveness of variety, previously discussed, means that those components that are more rather than less complex will tend to be the first that became linked to other components or levels within the system of greater complexity. A drift "upward" of components within the system follows from increases in development. New items (in general reflecting higher levels of complexity in their combination or fusion than older ones) tend to shift to components with more organized complexity or levels with greater integrated diversity.

Also, since all new items of variety taken on by any component reduce the level of organization of the component (but the greater the number of components and the higher the level of the organization of that variety, the less the reduction), those components acquiring variety that begins to approach its upper limit will tend to exchange that variety for redundant identities. These redundant identities reduce the total distribution of properties among the components. The latter means that components with less variety are more likely to exchange new variety for redundant identities, depending on the total amount of variety they hold. Components with little variety, of course, have the capacity to take on additional variety and are less likely to exchange it for redundant identities.

More complex components or levels with more integrated diversity are likely to hold rather than distribute variety for a longer period of time than those with less. The primary reason that new items of variety will be accumulated rather than distributed or exchanged by components of greater complexity is the greater probability of their using variety for producing additional items of variety. Their cost for retaining items of variety is, as has been indicated, less; the probability that such items of variety can be combined and fused is greater.[5]

In addition to accumulating variety, and thereby dampening the rate of decline in integration by delaying distribution, components also "integrate" new items of variety into new properties, distributing those properties rather than their parts. Thus, instead of two properties being distributed, causing diversity, two or more items are organized into one, and one property is distributed, containing the complexity of the two plus the additional complexity that derives from their combination or fusion. For the system as a whole the complexity of the properties is roughly the same but with less diversity, at least initially. For example, large economic organizations, rather than distributing new products, may keep them and use them to produce still other new products. This process, however, as well as transferring variety to other components, results in some loss in both diversity and variety.

With development, there are more points in the system—components and levels with both unique aggregations of variety and different amounts of variety. This increases the system's capacity to absorb new variety with less of a loss in integration. A large number of locations and points in the system means that there are more alternative places where new variety can fit, that is, be taken on with less disturbance. As a consequence, new variety entering a system can be shifted faster. First, the structural "distance" within the system that a new item of variety will have to move will be less, and the time required, accordingly, reduced. In part this is because the law of attractiveness of variety means that variety moves toward the next higher level. The more points in the system, the more probable that the next highest available level will be closer in terms of both complexity and interaction time. Second, with a large number of points in the system—differentiated components and levels-the greater the probability that any one point will be open to new variety in terms of its past acquisition sequence of its last new item of variety. Taking on new variety at any point in time reduces the propensity to take on another at the next point in time. As time passes and as the new variety becomes organized by the component, the probability of taking on a new item increases. Systems with more locations will have components and levels that have taken on new variety at different points in time, and thus have more locations that have organized their variety and are ready to take on additional, new variety.

The foregoing means that as the level of development of a system increases, its absorptive capacity for new variety increases; new variety will reduce the level of integration less, and the time required for integration is also less.

THE LOSS AND CONSERVATION OF VARIETY

As the system responds to new variety by shifting it to points in the system better able to absorb it (thus delaying diversity until it can be better integrated), there is a loss in variety and diversity. First, variety that takes time for distribution is in effect lost through delay. Delaying diversity, however, gains time as a resource for integration. Second, any movement of variety involves some loss by its mere transfer from the point of origin to a point of absorption. Third, if a new item of variety is held by a component and then later used to create a new item of variety by combining or fusing two or more items of variety, the potential of that item of variety, contributing to diversity and the production of new variety by other components is lost. Thus, the integrative responses to variety by delaying its transformation into system diversity results in some loss in producing new variety.

These losses are recoverable by certain compensating responses that tend to conserve variety for some future time. By delaying diversity through restricting distribution to components, variety is distributed and becomes diversity and similarities at a point in time when the components are better able to absorb it. Second, although variety is lost through movement, this loss is compensated for by cognitive representations of properties rather than the properties themselves. Thus transfer of object properties, and the loss ensuing from the transfer, can be recovered in part by coding these object properties into properties proper.[6] Third, the combination or fusion of a new item of variety before it is widely distributed does not preclude the deaggregation of that property. Such combinations, however, may forever preclude the use of some variety as an independent source of diversity. To the extent that the properties are not or cannot be deaggregated there is permanent loss in diversity and, consequently, in the potential variety in that if that variety had been distributed, it might have yielded different variety.

The delay, integration, and then distribution into diversity response of systems, using the organization of variety of components and the integration of diversity of levels as a resource for lack of systemwide integration does, however, speed up the integration of diversity in the long run. Thus, that variety that might have been lost to the system because of its lack of capacity to integrate the diversity that could have been generated by variety becomes a system property, an item of diversity in the long run. This leads to the conservation of variety.[7]

LIMITS TO INTEGRATION

For any level of diversity there are lower and upper limits to the level of integration. If the level of integration falls below the lower limit, the system will disintegrate or collapse. If the level of integration exceeds the upper limit, no new variety can be introduced, the processes of development will stop, and the system will developmentally stagnate. Thus, there is a range of values for both diversity and integration that will engage the dynamic of development. Below that range, there is collapse; above it, stagnation.

Because developmental systems are positive feedback systems, they necessarily cannot have their level of integration repeatedly fall to a previous level. Such would be the case if diversity reduces integration to level x, diversity is integrated at level x, and new variety reduces integration to level x-1; integration, then increases to level x. If this were to happen, there would be no increase in the level of diversity of the system. The system would be in a state of dynamic equilibrium.

The developmental process must be one where variety increases diversity at one point in time $(y+1)$, which reduces integration $(x-1)$ at another point in time; and diversity is reduced to $y > y + 1$; at future points in time integration must increase to $x > x + 1$. Thus, for development to continue across time, the level of integration cannot repeatedly fall at or below the level at some previous point in time.

For empirical social systems, however, there is a positive probability that the level of integration will indeed fall below some previous level, and, thus, also a positive probability that it will continue to fall below that level for several times in succession. The higher the level of development, however, the less the probability of decline and collapse, if only because there is more total integration to lose.[8] Furthermore, lower levels of integration reduce the probability of new items of variety being produced, and consequently the probability of successive instances of integration falling below some previous level. Thus, there is some probability that integration will decline, but as integration continuously falls below some previous point, the probability of still further reductions declines, because of the reduction in the probability of new variety.

Although the above may help explain why developmental systems are not likely to collapse and why all such systems do not in fact continue to develop, what must be shown is why, as the level of development increases, the probability of a system's integration falling below some previous level decreases.

The dynamics leading to integration, must proceed at a rate such that increases in diversity do not overcome it. First, just as variety, when distributed, can contribute to an exponential increase in diversity, the reduction in diversity from shifts in variety is also exponential. Diversity would decline to previous levels if integration did not occur. The initial increases in integration slow down the decrease in diversity, resulting from shifting variety to other components. As a consequence, diversity does not fall below the previous level. Second, as similarities increase along with diversity and as similarities increase the probability of integration, the probability of integration falling below previous levels, after an increase in both similarities and diversity, is reduced. Increasing similarities thus provide an increasing base line below which the level of integration is less and less likely to fall. Third, for the reasons presented above, as the rate of integration increases with development (and, in particular, because the number of points within the system to which new variety can be shifted increases), the time in which integration can fall below previous levels declines as well as the probability that it will.

The upper limit to integration is that point where the level of integration is such that the system stops to produce new variety. This will be posited as a theoretical assumption: Development ceases when the level of integration exceeds the level of diversity for two or more consecutive time intervals; it is the integration of diversity taking place across time that produces new variety. If the level of integration remains constant, then, by definition, there can be no new integrative responses leading to new variety. Once there is no new variety, and thus no additional diversity for two or more points in time, development will cease, and the system will, therefore, stagnate.

In addition to ceasing the production of new variety, generating the technological change necessary for development, as systems become more integrated, their "resistance" to "disturbing" variety will increase. This factor, is based on the absolute level of integration. The system is "too highly" integrated, and, consequently, the "force" of diversity must be strengthened to overcome the system's resistance to new variety.

Although at high levels of integration this resistance contributes to possible stagnation, what is theoretically critical for development is the integrative response, that is, increases in integration in response to new variety. It is that response, rather than the actual level of integration, that stimulates new variety and thus development. Systems can stagnate at low levels of integration.

Once a system, however, becomes totally integrated (1.00), no future integration is possible. And if it remains totally integrated for two or more intervals of system response time, there will be no further development. When this point is reached, the system is either transformed or it stagnates. By definition then, some system slack is necessary for development—slack which is defined as the amount of integration that is less than total integration.

THE DEVELOPMENTAL HISTORY OF SYSTEMS

An historical explanation of a system's development involves the deduction of the future development of the system by knowing how the system behaved developmentally in the past. These past points of observation would be system response intervals either an increase in diversity and a decrease in integration or an increase in integration and a decrease in diversity, rather than natural time intervals, such as years. This theory provides for deriving theoretically relevant units of time—the units of time that must be observed in order to explain past or future states of the system. These units of system response time are the number of points in natural time where diversity increased and integration decreased or where integration increased and diversity decreased. Three such system-response time units would enable some probability of projecting the direction of change-development, stagnation, or collapse. Furthermore, the higher the level of development, the fewer the real time intervals that define the system's theoretical time, the system response interval. The theory defines theoretically relevant historical periods, independent of chronological time.

A test of a theory is its ability to make historical predictions. A systemic theoretical approach allows predicting or retrodicting the states of the system from a few historical observations. The fewer the observations required for a full statement of all past and future states of the system, the more powerful the theory. This is one of the advantages of a system theory, incorporating time as an integral part of the theoretical statements. Theory and history in this sense become equivalent.

DEVELOPMENT AND SYSTEM ENTROPY

Systems are subject to negative entropy—the natural decrease in their level of integration as a function of time alone. Among the defining characteristics of social systems is that they can, through autonomous processes increase their level of integration, and therefore can overcome negative entropy. For developing systems, those that are continuously increasing and decreasing their integration, it is difficult to determine what proportion of the decrease is due to entropy and what to developmental dynamics. Once the process of development begins to become exponential, whatever might be posited as the magnitude of negative entropy would be negligible in comparison to the rate of increase in integration. Entropy, however, is an increasing function of the level of development of the system. Thus, on the one hand, entropy becomes an increasingly important factor in accounting for reductions in integration for more highly developed systems, and on the other, exponential increases in development will exceed any negative entropy.

For systems that are totally integrated, negative entropy might have several different implications. Negative entropy implies that no totally integrated system can remain totally integrated; in the long run, it will decline. The question is: will the slack introduced by entropy for highly or totally integrated systems activate developmental dynamics? This is improbable since what stagnates a system are successive states of no decrease and no increase in integration. Thus negative entropy for highly or totally integrated systems will run the systems down rather than activate the dynamics of development. System slack is a necessary but not sufficient condition for system development.

THE DYNAMICS OF INTEGRATING DIVERSITY: A SUMMARY

Figure 3 presents the dynamic of integrating diversity. The ordinate is scaled to reflect diversity as varying between 0.0 and 1.00, indicating the proportion of total diversity possible that has been attained, and integration as also varying between 0.0 and 1.00, according to the definition of integration. Thus, these two metrics can be compared.

The vertical lines delineate the system response intervals in real time, which decrease over time as the level development increases. The constant equal intervals on the abscissa indicate arbitrary units of real time, such as months or years.

In the figure the system starts at a level of integration and diversity of .5. This indicates some level of development, surely enough to have engaged the autonomous processes of development. Starting each equally, however, is only hypothetical and is

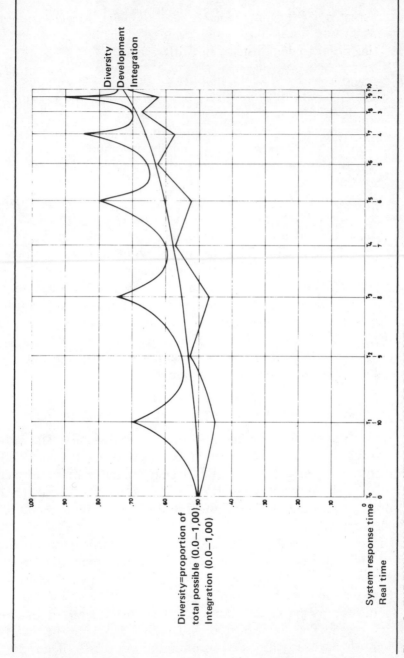

Figure 3: THE DYNAMIC OF THE INTEGRATION OF DIVERSITY

not consistent with the theory of development. Developmental systems should never have equal levels of both. It was chosen as a starting point to demonstrate their divergence.

Diversity increases exponentially and decreases exponentially but at a slower rate and not to the previous level, after integration begins to increase. Integration decreases and increases in a line approximating linear increases and decreases. As the level of both increases, the real time interval of the system response decreases.

The quantity of both integration and diversity, and hence development, is intended to be an average of the total amount of diversity and integration and an average of increases in diversity and integration. The point within each interval where diversity increases exponentially is the point at which new variety is introduced, again a hypothetical point, as at any point in time more than one new item of variety are being added.

The level of development is the middle line, between those of integration and diversity. Although it should be a smooth undulating curve, reflecting relative increases and decreases of integration and diversity, it is presented here as an increasing line, an estimated interpolation. It begins to show an exponential increase.

The Integration of Levels as a Process: An Overview

Systems organize their components into levels which can be differentiated on the basis of their number of components and their integration of variety. These levels provide the structure for integrating diversity derived from variety. Their formation, growth, and incorporation are, however, the consequence of increasing variety and diversity in the system. Thus variety, because of its integration as diversity, not only reduces the level of system integration but also generates differentiated levels within the system that are the structural requisite for the integration of diversity.

This is the cross-level dynamic of development. Its link to the integration of diversity closes the system loop, thus theoretically explaining developmental change in the nature of the components, on the one hand, and the integration of diversity, on the other.

With some level of and some increase in diversity, the components of a system become related on the principle of both their similarity and differences. Since both the similarities and the differences are few, but similarities predominate, components are linked primarily through their similarities. As social units acquire more and more properties, they pull away from those components which are primarily aggregations based on similarities and begin to become differentiated.

Once this process of differentiation begins, the following occur over time: (1) components within the system emerge as levels in which interaction among the components comprising a level is greater than their interaction outside of it; (2) as these levels acquire more and more variety and diversity within and as that variety becomes organized, components with less variety will be attracted to it (because of the law of the attractiveness of variety); (3) components initially transfer their variety to higher levels which are better able to absorb it in exchange for access to that variety; (4) as variety continues to be transferred upward, the components become disassociated from their membership in levels as they themselves continually take on new variety, which is transferred to still higher levels; (5) properties continue to be transferred to higher levels within the system and levels of components with even greater variety and organization of that variety emerge; and (6) in turn, additional variety is distributed to de-aggregating components. The logical conclusion of this process is that what remains are individuals as components and the system itself. All intermediate levels are absorbed by the system.

THE AGGREGATION OF COMPONENTS

With the distribution of variety, the existing components acquire properties which increase both their similarities to and differences from others. With a small number of total properties in the system, similarities are predominant. These similarities, because they are unequally distributed, form the basis for aggregating components. These aggregations are similar within and different from others.

The law that explains why both diversity and similarities increase (the law of aggregative diversity and inclusive similarity) states that those components that are both more similar and more different will tend to interact. One implication of this law is that those components that are similar in the qualities of their total number properties as well as their total number of properties are more likely to interact than those that are less similar in both the quality and quantity of properties. This component-to-component interaction across time creates the basis for association and bonding among the components. The consequence of the foregoing is that there are hierarchies of sets of components, differentiated on their total number of properties, on the one hand, and their number of similarities, on the other. This is the structural basis for differentiated levels within the system. It involves concentrations of components with similarities, both territorial and organizational.

As more variety is distributed to components, there are additional structural bases for the formation of aggregations of components depending on the abundance and the unequal distribution of these properties. If all of the components in the system have a particular property, then, of course, it cannot be a basis for aggregations of subsets. Furthermore, as the properties in part determine interaction, their initial distribution will have some permanence. There will be more momentum for interaction and exchange of properties within the aggregation than without.

The aggregation of components for societies means that there are broadly based sets of components, sharing one or a few properties and aggregating into interests and social classes setting one apart from another. With increases in the number of properties and their variety following some history of interaction within the configurations of interests, groups form, but generally they are smaller, less inclusive than the broadly based interest groupings. These groups, however, relate more properties of the components more intensely than do the interest groupings, and, consequently, they tend to be less inclusive. With further distributions of properties such groups, depending in part on the distribution of those same properties to other groups, organize on the basis of their interaction within and exclusion without. This results in the emergence of institutions and organizations of some complexity. These changes are one of the basic kinds of developmental changes— changes in the nature of components of developmental systems.

THE FORMATION AND EMERGENCE OF LEVELS

If the number of properties and new properties were to cease to enter the system or to cease to be distributed, the social system would freeze into more or less permanent sets of hierarchically organized components and segmented groups or groupings. These hierarchical levels would have minimal interaction with those above and below them; and the groups would have little across segment interaction. The loosening of these hierarchical and sectional cleavages can occur only with increased development or forced political action to break them down.

A higher level within the system is one that has at least one more item of variety than that of a lower level. Levels are, therefore, relational. For higher level aggregates this is a definition—any higher level must be more inclusive than a lower level, or in the language of this theory, must have more variety than lower levels. For systems and subsystems this is a law, implying that if a system does not have greater "variety" than any of its subsystems, then either the subsystem will "leave" the system or else the system will collapse for lack of control, one of the definitional requirements of a system vis-à-vis subsystems.[9] What must be shown in order to explain the emergence of levels of greater and greater variety is not only that there are such levels but also that such levels continue to acquire more variety vis-à-vis lower levels and thus continually become more inclusive, that is, share the properties of lower levels.

With a limited number of properties and variety, there are inequalities among the components. Those with relatively more variety have the potential for becoming or merging into higher and, indeed, the highest level within the system. This occurs because of the law of attractiveness of variety. The law of inclusive similarity that "likes will interact with likes" in terms of quality and quantity of similarities applies when there are limited properties. It yields aggregates of components. With some variety, components, in order to acquire more variety, will relate to, or exchange with, those components or levels with more variety. What variety they have will be exchanged for additional variety. Thus, in order to acquire more variety, components with less variety exchange or interact with those that have more with variety or at least equal variety plus one additional item of variety. The law of similarities, however, is still operative: the more similar the components, the more likely the interaction. The consequence of the relationship between the laws of attractiveness of variety and aggregative diversity means that components of one level are most likely to interact with those of the next highest level, then with the next highest level, etc., and are least likely to exchange with the level with the most or least variety.[10]

This means that there will be a hierarchical ordering of levels of components based on variety and, most importantly, the formation of intermediate groups or levels, those that deal with higher levels of complexity by transferring properties from lower levels. The expansion of these intermediate levels depends on both increases in the number and variety of properties and on the initial distribution.

Two additional factors contributing to these shifts in levels are, first, the upward migration of those properties of the most complexity, often, as was discussed, those items that are newer, and, second, the drift of components of the greatest complexity toward the higher levels within the system, often joining or being incorporated by them. The drift upward of both variety and of those components with relatively more variety impoverishes variety at lower levels. Initially, this impoverishment affects the lowest levels of components to the decided benefit of intermediate levels; then, of course, the same consequence affects the intermediate levels. If towns lose to cities initially, then cities lose to the nation eventually, and then the nation to the global system, ultimately.[11]

With the establishment of linkages between levels, variety is exchanged for access to variety, the potentiality that a lower level component can acquire variety at some future point in time. Actual variety is exchanged for future variety, and exchange of properties for accessibility is a positive function of cross-level integration. Furthermore, access to variety is more important for the lower level components, as their capacity for holding variety is limited. With time, this capacity increases as their existing variety becomes organized. Access relationships are, however, a basis for dependency relationships and lead to patterns of non-reciprocal relationships that inhibit exchange.

Access to variety held by levels within the system that are increasing their variety and exchanges across levels explain the process of differentiation and specialization. As variety increases, it is accumulated by certain components and forms the basis for components relating to other components with different types of variety. Similar components are concentrated and identical properties are accumulated in exchange for access to variety. This is manifest in specialization in production and access to variety in consumption. The process of differentiation and specialization does not, however, explain why higher level components and levels within the system do not specialize but rather "diversify." Diversification reflects their higher level position in the system, which is a consequence of variety that they have and are accumulating.

THE DEAGGREGATION OF COMPONENTS

With increasing variety, diversity, and the total number of properties, existing components begin to differentiate. This process of separation from other components and integration with the system continues until the deaggregatable component of the social system is all that is left. It is at this point in development that individuals emerge as dominant components of the system and become the proper focus for predicting the behavior of the system.

The first and critical factor leading to deaggregation of components is the upper limit to each component's properties, including levels of components. As was seen in the previous chapter, this upper limit forces the system to distribute properties or the system must increase the number of its components. Excluding transfers of variety outside of the system, the basic dynamic of increasing system size or the number of components in a closed system is to deaggregate its components, and the most numerous of potential components are individuals.[12]

As individuals begin to acquire variety, their variety tends to exceed that of the existing aggregations of components of which they are members. They pull away from these components and relate to levels within the system on the basis of their variety. As they pull away, there is initially a breakup of smaller aggregates, such as local communities, and later of larger intermediate level aggregates, such as interest groups. Components, or individuals, can begin to relate to that level within the system that is most similar and different to them. As more and more properties are

rather than reconciling conflicting differences. What conflicts there are take place with other systems that are different.

THE TRANSFORMATION OF COACTION SYSTEMS INTO INTERACTION SYSTEMS

The theory provides no theoretical explanation of why coaction systems are transformed into developmental systems. An historical account rather than an explanation, as defined in the introduction, can be indicated. The theoretical basis of the historical account would involve open system models, which are protypical for co-action systems. What would have to be shown, or accounted for, is how a social system that does not generate variety begins at some point not only to add occasional items of variety, but also to do so at a continually increasing rate.

Four general kinds of factors, exogenous to this theory, can be used to account for a coaction system acquiring a sufficient number of items of variety such that it "grows" variety rather than reproduces similarity.

(1) There are random factors that from time to time generate techno-
    logical changes, and these changes accumulate sufficiently to produce
    additional variety at a continually expanding rate.

(2) Variety is generated as adaptive responses to changes in the biophysi-
    cal environment.

(3) Variety is introduced by contact, even hostile contact, with other
    systems.

(4) The logic of the coaction systems is such that once it reaches a cer-
    tain size, the creation of variety is stimulated.

Whatever be the most suitable account for most cases or what-ever factors explain the most historical variance, three historical facts stand out:

(1) Only a few of the historically identifiable social systems exist today.

(2) Some social systems have persisted to this day as relatively stubborn,
    coaction systems, but these systems tend to be relatively isolated.

(3) Most basic changes in social systems were brought about by external
    penetration from other systems, sometimes gradual and peaceful, but
    frequently forceful and hostile.

What would be theoretically interesting to say about the transformation of coaction systems is that there is a size-variety dynamic. A system cannot cope with, even import, additional items of variety if it is of a certain size relative to its existing "variety," all of which is distributed into similarities or "uniformities." Systems would reach an upper limit of their size for their variety and would have to take on additional items of variety. If they do not grow, they collapse. Thus, coaction systems, given a certain amount and kind of variety, have size-environment variety equilibrium points. When for whatever reasons, even happenstance ones, the biophysical environment is benign enough to allow uninterrupted growth, the system will sooner or later reach its size limit. This limit could be broken only with an increase in variety.[14]

INTERACTION SYSTEMS

Interaction systems are based on the principle of similarities and differences. They are interaction systems because components relate to one another and change each other. As this interaction generates new variety, these are developmental systems, which, if they continue to acquire new properties, can be described by the process of development.

The primary systemically relevant activity of the components is production. A primary means for increasing the system's diversity is through exchange. Exchanges not only increase the system's diversity but also increase the probabilities of creating new variety, which is then multiplied and exchanged. Since production if the primary activity of interaction systems, the decisive social roles are those of occupation; and since accumulation of properties is critical, major forms of social differentiation are property, income, and class, reflecting both possession of properties and access to variety. Exchange is central to the process of development, and since it involves detaching properties from components and moving them across time and space, these systems are dominated by object properties.

The nature of the components of interaction systems continuously changes. As has been indicated, they are classes, aggregates, groups, organizations, and institutions. Subsystems are formed and are absorbed by others. Levels within the system are differentiated and become more encompassing. Individuals emerge as autonomous actors. Depending on the level of development, there is a mixture of kinds and types of components which are forming and being absorbed by others.

In social relations, there are hierarchies based on both number and kind of social properties; there is conflict among groups; there are cleavages across sectors. If these relationships remain dominant, there will be little development. What is essential for development is the transfer of properties among components. This can happen by political force, conflict, and exchange, all forms of interaction among the components. Such relationships, again, change; conflict among components evolves into exchanges; components lower in the hierarchy advance upward.

Over time, as the level of development increases, there is a tendency toward greater autonomy of the components, greater equality among them, and, consequently, more reciprocity in exchange. Furthermore, the rate of exchange increases as well as the quantity of items in process of exchange.

There are not only differentiated groups and classes in interaction systems but also differentiated sectors, such as the economic and political sectors. Political matters become important and, thus, political participation. The structures of political decision-making involve aggregations of interests, reconciliations of differences, force to obtain compliance with decisions, and opposition. Institutions increase their control, and political institutions gain dominance.

Although the foregoing is a brief selection of some of the manifold characteristics of interaction systems (additional discussion is presented in the following chapters), such systems, of course, contain characteristics of coaction systems, and with development begin to take on the characteristics of transaction systems. It is also possible to distinguish types of interaction systems that differ according to the number of properties, the variety of properties, and the integration of diversity. For example, at the low levels, conflicts and cleavages are more apparent than exchanges; at high levels, exchanges are more apparent than conflicts. Thus, within interaction systems both the components and the relationships among them are continuously changing, and from time to time these changes may result in major discontinuities in the nature of the system. Whether these discontinuities will result in further development or the abortion of development depends on the consequent distribution of properties and the integration of the system.

THE TRANSFORMATION OF INTERACTION SYSTEMS

Whatever might be the particular historical course of a system, the formal point at which interaction systems are transformed is defined by both the maximum levels of diversity and its integration. This is the logical consequence of development. It is a developmental change of magnitude and moment. It contrasts with the more mixed qualitative changes of interaction systems. It yields a far-reaching set of qualitative changes.

In addition to system transformation defined as the maximum number of components (individuals), the maximum attainment of potential diversity, and near complete or total integration, there is the theoretical point of time. As the intervals of real time required to produce variety, generate diversity, and integrate components are continuously reduced, the point where these intervals begin to approach instantaneous time is another logical conclusion of the developmental process that defines the point at which interaction systems are transformed.

These are logical rather than empirical points. In any system, even those at the highest levels of development, there is always less than total diversity, some time required to integrate diversity, and some system slack. The theoretical point, does, however, provide a basis for analyzing particular systems and approximating when particular systems are in the process of being transformed.

At the point of transformation, the developmental processes described cease. There are no more components to deaggregate, no more levels that are absorbing variety, and no more dynamics of integrating diversity. What takes place are flows of properties in near instantaneous time.[16]

TRANSACTION SYSTEMS

Transaction systems are dominated by the principle of differences rather than similarities. Whereas in growth systems, the components are characterized by identities and similarities, and in interaction systems by similarities and differences, in transaction systems the components are characterized only by differences, unique combinations of variety. The similarities reside at the level of the system. The system is the focal point of similarities; the components of differences.

The dominant behavior of transaction systems is the flow of properties proper rather than the exchange of object properties. These properties flow, since they do not occupy a unique place in time and space, and, thus, they are free of social constraints. They flow through the networks of the system rather than from one component to another. The relationships among components are, therefore, through the system itself; they are indirect. Since the properties are in a state of flow, in process rather than in possession by particular components, every component has access to them. The form or substance of these properties is that of symbols; their flow is characterized as communications. Their use and distribution do not detract from their use by other components. Rather, their use enhances their "value."

The components of transaction systems are individuals. Intermediate groups and levels within the system have been absorbed by the system. What remains, consequently, are individuals and their variety and the system with its networks of linkages and its variety. The variety of the system, although exceeding the sum total of the variety of its components because of its capacity to store properties proper, is the potential variety of every components and, thus, a similarity among all components.

Because each individual as a component will be near its capacity of variety, there is ipso facto equality among the individuals. This equality is not, however, qualitative equality in the sense of the same kinds of properties. It is equality in terms of numbers of properties proper and the uniqueness of the combination of the variety of those properties. Thus social relationships are symmetrical and do not form the structural social basis for hierarchies and conflict.

Since the system is responsive to the behavior of individuals and since it is possible for all individuals to satisfy their preferences, there is no central decision–making center. In interaction systems, the center acts as surrogate for system integration; in transaction systems, when the system is fully developed, there need be no center that acts to allocate properties and integrate components. Properties are virtually unlimited; and integration nearly complete. The participation of individuals in the system derives from their behavior, and their behavior alters the state of the system. Thus, there is a merger of the sectors—the political, social, and economic. Since any act of an individual can influence the state of the system, every individual act is political.

In interaction systems, variety is both the source of development and the danger to the integration of the system; in transaction systems, new properties proper are almost immediately absorbed and stored in the system or transferred to components. New variety thus comes about as a turnover of existing properties which are transferred to the system. Because properties proper are not constrained by space and time, the system has almost unlimited capacity to store and retrieve all past variety. And because the greater the amount of variety, the greater the probability of creating new variety, the rate of producing new variety results in rapid turnover of properties almost continuously.

The Level and Rate of Development: A Summary

One major consequence of the dynamics of development is that as the level of development increases, the rate of development increases. This relationship obtains for interaction systems to the point of their transformation, when exponential increases have little meaning as the rate of increases in variety is rapid.

The rate of development increases as a function of the level of development for a combination of reasons presented throughout this chapter. Each factor contributes to an accelerating increase in development. Among the factors that have been presented, the major ones will be summarized. First, as the level of diversity within the system increases, the probability of producing new variety increases. This implies that new variety will emerge in shorter periods of real time. Second, as the integration of the system increases, the time taken to integrate new variety decreases. Third, as there are increases in the numbers of levels within the system, the time required for a property to move from one component to another decreases. Fourth, the sooner properties are transferred, the sooner will be the response of an increase in integration, and the production of new variety.

These quantitative increases in development explain the changing relationships between level and rate, itself a developmental change, emanating from the processes of development.

NOTES

1. Up to the point of diminishing diversity. It is assumed that distribution of object properties and diffusion of properties proper both take time.

2. Systemic conflict is derived from the developmental dynamics. It is a consequence of integrating diversity and is essential to the continuation of development.

3. This relationship between the level and rate of inventions and innovations is, of course, manifest in cross-national comparisons. Per capita patents and inventions are less relevant than the level and rate. In recent years new patents per capita may be declining in advanced industrialized countries. In part this is due to the shift from "hardware" inventions to "software" fusions, which are difficult to specify and almost impossible to keep from others. Technology II is also historically confirmed in the exponential decline over the past centuries in the time-cost-distance constraints on the transportation of goods and people.

4. Political intervention can correct the destabilizing effects of development. In general, the lack of integration of diversity defines some limits to governmental intervention. For developing systems with lags in integration this may mean intervention to increase integration by curtailing variety and diversity and forcing integration through hierarchical organizations. Although the theory states the conditions under which such governmental and other forms of intervention can take place and be effective, it cannot predict whether or in what ways governments will act.

5. Acquisition of variety, however, is no guarantee that it will be used to produce additional variety. The variety may be retained for "power" or position or simply consumption.

6. This is one aspect of system memory.

7. The storage capacity of the system at higher levels of development is another factor to be discussed. The capacity of the system to take on variety rather than reject it increases with the level of development, contributing to one of the basic derived laws of development: as the level of development increases, the rate of development also increases.

8. This raises the issue of whether more or less developed systems are vulnerable to disintegration. These theoretical arguments support a position that it is neither the most nor the least developed but those beginning the process of development change. The analogy to highly specialized species is not appropriate. Development is integrated diversity and high level of integrated diversity provides ever expanding alternatives in addition to growing capacity for their use. Less developed social systems have few but highly reenforced relationships, which are difficult either to erode or destroy. In systems that are beginning to develop, new relationships are weak but yet erosive of the established relationships.

9. This is the "law of requisite variety," discussed in Chapter 2. Depending on its interpretations, it may be a definition rather than an empirical law. Its "falsifiability" is difficult to state.

10. These laws, incidentally, also explain why components with the most variety are more likely to interact with components with equivalent levels of variety outside of the system rather than with components with less variety within it. In part this also explains such phenomena as the circulation of the elites and greater trade among the most developed countries exchanging more goods with the least developed. The same logic applies to relationships among regions within countries and accounts for the international orientation of the most developed regions and the dependency relationship of the least developed regions on the most developed regions.

It is a more general explanation than "dependency theory" in international relations. Both the dependency relationships of less "developed" countries on the more developed and the penetration of the most developed countries into "developed" areas, urban areas, in less "developed" countries follow from the laws of attractiveness of variety. Dependency theory thus should be seen as part of developmental processes at the global, international level. Such structural relationships invite exploitation, but it probably would persist for some time despite massive political efforts to reverse this pattern.

11. Under certain circumstances development involves zero-sum exchanges: one level gains at the expense of others. What this discussion implies is that for some time, intermediate levels impoverish lower levels, but they in turn are impoverished by still higher levels. This process continues to a point where individuals and the "system" gain at the expense of all intermediate levels.

12. Although these statements have the overtones of functional explanation ("in order to, it must") such explanations in this discussion are either avoided or translated into a systemic explanation. What is being said is that the "weight" of properties triggers some distribution. If that does not happen, then the developmental dynamics will cease to operate. Such a statement, it can be argued, may not be overtly teleological, which is a characteristic of functional explanation (explaining an event in terms of its consequences), but it is not clearly functional. What really is at issue is the assumption of upper limits. If that assumption were not made, then one "component" could absorb all of the properties and variety, becoming by itself the developmental system. Again to exclude this possibility, an assumption, such as that of upper limits, must be used. If not, then the theory would end up in an interesting philosophical paradox, similar to that of the "universal set being a member of itself," rather than an empirical theory.

13. This description, as well as that of the other two types, is characteristical of "ideal types" for which there are no clear instances. Thus, these characteristics must be evaluated in general terms rather than from their fit with specific cases.

14. In these types of systems the "value" of the individual can be defined in terms of either their reproductive potential or their contribution to maintaining the family units.

15. Such an explanation would be structurally similar to a functional explanation. It would be a version of human ecology with concepts such as size, growth, environment, and equilibrium.

16. The focus of the theoretical analysis, therefore, is an interaction system whose behavior is determined by developmental dynamics.

PART II

DEVELOPMENTAL ACTIVITIES:
PRODUCTION AND DISTRIBUTION

The three chapters in Part I dealt with general relationships among properties of components and systems. These general developmental dynamics need to be interpreted in terms of activities that, in effect, "drive" the development of social systems.

Chapter 4 outlines how item objects and properties proper come about. They take shape in social systems through production, although what production is, depends on the level of development. Production in a low state of development is oriented to reproducing identities of object properties. In a higher state, object properties and properties proper, both identities and differences, are produced. At a high level of development, most of what is produced are different properties.

The sheer number of properties and their variety, however, do not result in diversity or its integration unless those properties are distributed. This is the second basic social activity: distribution. Distribution of properties affects production and the production in turn determines the structure of distribution.

In coaction systems the units of production and distribution are coterminous, leading to system level properties that are aggregates of the properties of the components. In interaction systems object properties dominate and move in limited networks from barter to market exchange. In transaction systems properties proper dominate and move in the network of the system. Both chapters are organized in terms of these three basic types of systems.

Chapter 4

THE PRODUCTION

OF SYSTEM PROPERTIES

In the theoretical perspective so far presented, the fundamental unit of behavior is some movement across time and space, or more accurately, a move across space in time. For social systems these movements originate from the objects that move—individuals. Not all movements by individuals, not even those movements that are individually based are social. They are social only if they take place in a defined social context or a social system. This also holds for certain nonhuman or inanimate movements. They too are social if they occur in a social system. All other movements can be considered parts of other kinds of systems.

Two criteria define social behavior: (1) the "basic" components of the system are individuals; and (2) there are some relationships among those individuals such that a unit of movement of one has some probability of affecting other individuals, at least some of the time. Movement as social behavior takes place in a range of systems: in simple systems, such as a family, and in complex systems, such as an industrialized state. Increases in the complexity of the networks to which these movements are linked is one general manifestation of development.

As the production of identical and new object properties and properties proper is necessary to development, those social processes that transform movements into properties of social systems, and particularly into developmental change must be explained. What there is, empirically, to start with in any social system is some act of individuals (whether pushing a cart or a button), in some place, at some time. Some consequences of some of these movements under certain conditions are developmental changes. Developmental change will affect how the next unit of movement will affect developmental change.

Production and Participation

Production is activity (movement) that transforms any item, object property, or property proper, into another item that is either identical to (an identity) or different from (a difference) other properties in the system.[1] The developmental "value" of production is derived from its contribution to an increase in the similarity or diversity of the system, which involves distribution (the focus of the following chapter).

Participation is that behavior of the components that has some impact on the state of the system. In this definition, all behavior of components that is linked to the system and affects it, however small and probable that effect, is participation. In a narrow sense, participation is conscious activity of individuals and groups that is intended to lead to desired changes in the state of the system.

The relationship between production and participation depends on the context of the system—whether it is a coaction system, where production is the reproduction of the units, an interaction system, where production is directed to multiplying object properties, or a transaction system, where production is the creation of properties proper. In interaction systems production is the primary form of participation of individuals and components. The impact of the components on the system through productive activities is, however, limited, segmented, and indirect. System-component linkages are separated from primary production activities. In transaction systems, productive activities become direct participation in the system. Participation is tied to the production of properties proper.

Production and Participation in
Coaction Systems

As production and participation have been defined, coaction systems have neither. This discussion of coaction systems is presented in order to define and contrast production and participation in interaction and transaction systems.

As coaction systems have been defined, there is no individual or component differentiation. The basic component-system linkage is that of aggregation. The contribution of a component to the properties of the system lies in its accumulation of identical items. Since there is no differentiation among components, any single component is as effective as any other.[2] Any individual can speak for the system. As the system does not take on variety, participation to change the state of the system is meaningless.

Although there is a participatory structure that links all components aggregatively and on certain issues to the collective fate and the survival of the system, there is no participation, defined as individual or group behavior that changes the state of the system. Participatory behavior in these structures is symbolic, involving the reaffirmation and reenforcement of existing affective ties. Since the social structure of these growth systems is largely that of specific components acting in concert (coaction) or in similar ways with almost no interdependence, symbolic participation maintains those ties to the aggregative collectivity. Examples of this include festivities, rituals, and group expression.

Symbolic participation is an essential social activity of social coaction systems. Without repetitive expression of shared similarities, the system of coaction and cooperation would weaken because it lacks structures of interdependence. The component members of the collectivity are, in short, tied together by aggregative structures based on a few similarities and strong attachments to those similarities.

Production in Interaction Systems

Production in interaction systems is both component intrinsic, retained by the component, and extrinsic, linked to other components. With development, the proportion that is extrinsic to that which is intrinsic continually increases. As what is extrinsic becomes linked to the system, it becomes involved in the processes of developmental change.

A primary activity in interaction systems is production for exchange. There has to be some kind and amount of diversity for exchange. Thus, for there to be any reason or logic to the reproduction of multiple identical object properties, there must be some level of diversity going beyond the sharing of identities that dominates coaction systems. If there are only aggregative relational properties of identities and, thus, near equality, there can be neither dependence nor interdependence.

Production at low levels of exchange involves the multiplication of few identical object properties. The multiplication of these redundant identities is the structural foundation for interaction systems. The production of quantities—those items that are not needed for component survival, intrinsic production—becomes the basis for component extrinsic relationships.

At low levels of development diversity can be rapidly achieved through the multiplication of the same items and their distribution. Many items of the same thing can be distributed to provide diversity. Components with many items of the same thing—several horses, many automobiles, etc.—become increasingly involved in exchange processes, those activities that result directly in increasing diversity.

The capacity of some components to produce and/or accumulate large amounts of object properties of the same kind accounts for the rapid growth in material inequality with initial increase in production. What is present are differences in quantity with little variety. Because items are limited at the first stages, when the production of identical object properties predominates, there is substantial material inequality.

FROM THE PRODUCTION OF IDENTITIES TO THE PRODUCTION OF VARIETY

The basic question is why does the production of identical object properties give way to the production of variety? Why should a household give up grain for paper? Here it is necessary to use a theoretically exogenous factor—a system value—although up to this point, the dynamics of development have not formally included values.[3] Aside from individual, group, or organizational preferences, variety increases the social unit's value to a developmental social system. In order to relate to other components in the system, it is necessary for a component to share at least one property in common; and the greater the number of shared similarities and differences with other components, the higher the probability that there will be social interaction. The social position of the component is based on the extent to which it shares the variety of the system.

The above can be generalized: additional redundant object properties contribute a decreasing amount to the system's total "social base" (how many items any component can exchange with how many other components); each item that yields a difference contributes an increasing amount to the "social base." As was discussed, initial additional identical object properties contribute to the variety of the component as well as to the diversity of the system. After a certain accumulation of these identities is attained, the distinctiveness which a component acquires from still additional items of that identity gradually declines to a point that any other additional item adds neither to component variety nor to system diversity (law of diminishing diversity). By contrast, any different item acquired by a component adds to the system's diversity and to the component's variety, increasing its social base or distinctiveness, although not linearly. The reason for this function being nonlinear but monotonic is that the distinctiveness added by different properties depends on the context of the system, on how many other components have the same item.

The above is the basis for the general law that drives exchange in interaction systems: the marginal increase of the component's propensity to exchange redundant identical object properties for items of difference.[4] Thus, for example, having two horses might be distinctive, having three less distinctive, having four still less, etc. Each additional horse will increase the propensity of the component to exchange a horse for some item that contributes to its variety, thereby increasing the system's diversity. For the system as a whole this means that the sheer multiplication of items of identity will increase the total diversity of the system to a certain limit through the exchanges that follow. Diversity follows exchange, since exchanges result in a distribution of properties, as well as in an increase in the variety of components.

The multiplication of identical object properties defines that part of a producing component that is extrinsic. The result of even rudimentary exchange, or movement of object properties from one component to another, is that the diversity of the system will be increased.

The initial structures of exchange are bilateral or barter relationships, in which one object property is literally exchanged for another. There is a specific target of exchange, another component. A rudimentary structure that facilitates barter activity is the bazaar, where many bilateral exchanges can take place at one time and at one place. The use of money expands bilateral or pairwise exchange relationships into exchange networks. These exchange networks are limited, of course, to those who recognize the currency of exchange. The exchange networks, at a certain point of elaboration, become markets, which through the process of integration become more and more inclusive, and which because of the commonality of preferences underlying them, become increasingly encompassing.

What is important concerning exchange is that it acts as a stimulus to production. As was argued, the greater the number of exchanges at any point in time, the greater the probability of an increase in exchanges at the next point in time. What is of interest is not the percentage increase each year, but rather the total increase from year to year, which for most highly industrialized countries manifests an exponential growth most of the time.

THE ORGANIZATION OF PRODUCTION

With the elaboration of interaction systems, there is organization of productive activities. Foremost among this organizational growth is the separation of productive movement of items through space and in time. The movement of items in interaction systems becomes almost as involved a process as producing them. In highly elaborated interaction systems, the number of people employed in moving object properties or diffusing properties proper—sales, transportation, etc.—will begin to equal or even exceed the number working to produce those items.

The organization of production involves reducing particular movements into smaller units. The greater this reduction, the greater the similarity among kinds of movements and the greater the efficiencies that can be obtained from repeating these movements. The more simple or elementary the unit of movement, the more easily it can be simulated and then replaced by inanimate or mechanical systems in which repetition dominates. Thus, the organization of production means breaking down activities into identical groups of movements, complex movements into simple, repetitive ones.

As production is divided into smaller but more units of movement, there is increased need for coordination in combining them. These coordination activities are at the focus of the organization of production, beginning with the emergence of managerial activities. Differentiation of activities within producing organizations leads to organizational specialization and, thus, to the organization of exchanges among them. The process of production becomes elaborated with exchanges among organizations, some sets of which can dominate whole sectors of production. These exchanges are exchanges for production.

Producing organizations for some period of time "develop" in a manner parallel to social systems. First, there is some form of growth or simple expansion, increasing the capacity to produce multiple items of the same kind. Second, these expanding systems increase the variety of their production by incorporating additional units of variety. Thus, although there is less and less specialization of organizations of production as they incorporate variety, there is more and more specialization of the components within them. The amount of component specialization possible is, however, a function of the complexity of the entity being produced.

Some producing organizations expand more rapidly than others and incorporate existing organizations or units that are producing similar items. With such differentials in expansion, one or a few units can dominate the production of one or several object properties. If this expansion continues, there will be clashes with those producing units that are producing the same items. At this point there is competition for control over one or several items. With competition begins further diversification of the items produced by organizations, not only to insure their stability in the face of competition but also as a consequence of the logic of expansion itself. With the introduction of variety into organizations, there are reductions in classical measures of efficiency, such as input/output measures, which can be offset by still further specialization of components within the organization. The trade offs for inefficiencies of size and scale are twofold: increased organizational stability in the sense of prototypical ecological systems (the greater the variety, the greater the stability vis-à-vis the environment) and greater efficiences of the producing unit as a whole. Increased efficiency obtains even though the number of decisions required for coordination increases. The decision costs per unit of production will, however, increase only slightly or may actually decrease with increasing complexity of the producing organization. Also, the investments that can be made in each decision, for example in careful planning per unit produced, will be greater, and thus on the average, their quality should be higher. This kind of expansion continues to a point where the organization becomes systemwide.

PRODUCING UNITS: THEIR IMPACT ON DEVELOPMENT

The consequences of the expansionistic logic of organized units of production for developmental change are several. Three are decisive:

(1) their contribution to a shift in levels of aggregation of the social systems in general;

(2) their stimulation of the flow of goods and ideas; and

(3) their transformation from the production of simple properties to that of complex ones.

First, the process of integration involves the inclusion of components into levels of greater variety within the system. The logic of expansion of organizations of production in effect pushes certain components into system levels, however incipient, of greater complexity. For example, individuals working in an organization in a small locality become at least conscious of the level of greater complexity with which the organization deals, such as manufacturing boats and the state of markets abroad. Interdependence with systems and levels of greater scale become obvious as one unit producing somewhere will be dependent on supplies and markets elsewhere. The basic point of large scale systems extending their size by integrating their source of supply and their markets, speaks to the logic of integrating diversity, even though in producing units at lower levels, this may touch only a small proportion of their properties.

Second, with the integration of organized units of production, changes in the nature of movements of items take place. Rather than the classical exchange pattern, where an item stops for a time and is "held or possessed" by a component, object properties within producing organizations have no component home. Rather, they move freely throughout the organization according to where they can contribute to conscious organizational goals. Within the organization, there is flow rather than exchange among the components, leading both to a higher level of diversity at any point in time as well as a higher level integration. As these organizations grow in size, the proportion of their total properties that is in a state of flow rather than in process of being exchanged continually increases. This is prototypical for the next type of macrodevelopmental systems, the transaction system.

Third, as the producing organization diversifies or increases both its complexity and size, it increases its capacity for shifting its production from identical items to different ones. This occurs for several reasons. The amount of variety required for producing any property proper, a new idea, is substantial. Rather than putting together several parts, or object properties, fragments of many ideas must be isolated and then fused into a new property proper, a new idea. These new ideas include both designs for the materialization of new sets of object properties and knowledge that can be distributed throughout the organization. Furthermore, the resources and capacity for allocating effort to producing new items, thereby increasing the organization's variety, are increased at high levels of complexity and size. In an exchange environment, these organizations will have to trade off their production of identities in the current market for investments to increase their variety for future markets. Also, as these organizations expand, they encounter in their environment items that are new to them. Each item that they encounter offers an opportunity for incorporation and an increase in their variety.

Highly organized units of production to some extent have a

structure similar to both ecological and developmental systems—
first increasing size, then variety, then size, then variety, etc., and
in some respects integrating their diversity and adding to it.

INVENTIONS, PRODUCTIVITY, AND DEVELOPMENT

Inventions are the combination of object properties into new
ones, adding to the variety of the system. The rate of inventions
increases as the diversity of the components and its integration
increase: a water pump and steam, a steam engine and a cart,
etc.[5] Inventions are thus a production of variety. As was elaborated, their multiplication and distribution initially contribute
more to the diversity than the similarity of the system. As this
multiplication continues, the invented variety begins to increase
similarity more than diversity.

Because of this, the rate of increase in the combination of
existing object properties into new ones will decline at some point
in the process of producing identical object properties. Qualitative
improvements of existing object properties will continue with
marginal additions of differences. New variety entering the system
will increasingly become properties proper.

One way of measuring productivity in industry is by the value,
or other measures of total output per hour of labor. There are,
of course, different interpretations of productivity due to several
controverted factors: technology, labor intensification, and the
organization of work. In terms of this definition of production,
productivity can be increased by reducing the number of movements required to produce an item. Productivity, or output per
movement, can be increased by the organization of movements,
the way in which various parts are put together. Despite the organization of work, working intensely, or the amount of investment
in technology, there are developmental factors that lead to increased productivity. These productivity factors are extrinsic to
the producing of organizations in that they involve its scale and
the scale of the system of which it is a component.

First, as mentioned, with increased organizational scale the
actual cost for organizational decisions per unit produced is proportionally reduced. A decision of a large scale organization, or
indeed a large scale society, is for all components rather than a

few. In addition, the number of people or components involved in these decisions can be absolutely increased, a greater variety of talents brought in, more time taken—all factors that may lead to better quality decisions—at a lower per component cost.[6]

Second, products that are incorporated into larger scale systems simply affect more other things than those incorporated into smaller scale ones. Thus, with a large market, or within a large producing organization, or within systems of great scale, any act has much greater ramifications, greater impact. This factor is in part related to the concept of economies of scale.

Third, with scale, as will be discussed, there are smaller fluctuations, and they tend to even out. This is an inherent part of the logic of large scale systems. A large scale system has the advantage that any act within the system (e.g., an engineering decision in a large corporation vs. one in a small shop) is likely to make more of an absolute difference to the system but less of a relative difference to the total operations of the system; the decision has less of a total impact on stability. Any fluctuation makes more of an absolute difference but, relative to all other things, less of an impact.

Productivity, with the elaboration and development of exchange structures, increases whether or not the input-output ratio declines. Development increases productivity and vice versa. Productivity increases development by increasing both the items of similarity and diversity until productive activities shift to the context of transaction systems.

Participation in Interaction Systems

Participation in interaction systems takes on some of the characteristics of participation defined as having some impact on the state of the system. Some forms of behavior (e.g., political behavior) are purposeful acts directed to changing the state of the system. By and large, however, in interaction systems the behavior of the components that changes the state of the system is indirect and not purposeful. Specific characteristics of interaction systems, however, determine what is participation and what is not.

With the expansion of variety and diversity, there is component differentiation. Initially, both similarities and differences among components increase, but rather slowly. There are both shared identities and differences, and the identities are the basis of interests and social classes. The differences among aggregates are the foundation for participation of groups and institutions. If they are not responded to in some way by the system, they result in substantial cleavages and fragmentation within the society.

A major change following the acquisition of some differences, especially of properties proper, is the differentiation of the individual from groups and social organizations. In rural areas where the organization of production is dominated by the dynamics of ecological systems, individuals have fixed positions in physical and social space, and the basic components of the system are institutions, classes, and territorial aggregations. With development brought about through changes in the nature of production, individuals begin to separate from these institutions and to acquire rudimentary forms of their own identity, including names, occupations, and other combinations of differences.[7]

Despite this, however, institutions and groups are superordinate to individuals. Individuals confront the reality that political parties, production organizations, interest groups, and class or other interests dominate. Some individuals are members of both the system and of one or more of these groups of a polity. But any effective participation comes about by activity in these organizations rather than individually.

Physical and social mobility strengthens the role of individuals in the system. Mobility in interaction systems is a direct function of the development of the system, on the one hand, and the number of similar and different properties of the individual (variety), on the other. The greater the variety of individuals and the more developed the system, the more likely that they can move to different places in the system, or indeed, out of the social system. With increases in individual variety, the hold of groups and institutions on individuals weakens, a prerequisite for the emergence of another type of participation.

Participation for individuals in interaction systems, depending on their level of development, is characterized by the following:

(1) membership in a variety of institutions and some participation in them;

(2) a few specific, although weak, structural linkages with the system as a whole (e.g., voting);

(3) a clear distinction between public and private behavior; and

(4) subordination of individual interests, preferences, and desires to the group.

For interaction systems, increases in participation have the following characteristics: an explicit and differentiated set of collective decision-making institutions (the polity); reconciliation or compromise of differences in decisions; and intense levels of participation which are either ignored or repressed through coercion. As a consequence of the latter, there are attempts, sometimes successful, to replace the existing social system and to establish one that is radically discontinuous.

Production activity, especially that of multiplying identical items in interaction systems, is largely divorced from participation Production has a substantial impact on the development of the system. But the primary purpose of production is perceived simply as producing more items and increasing the capacity to do so. Participation in the sense of component-system linkages that can change the state of the system is indirect and not purposeful. Because of this, side payments (material or ideological incentives) are required for participation. There is little direct individual satisfaction from participating in changing the system through the production. At higher levels of development, the perceived purposes of productive activity begins to extend beyond the mere multiplication of items to social and political activities.[8]

Involvement in exchange structures, such as the market, is largely an indirect and limited means of affecting the system, almost entirely unconscious. Although purchasing or selling in the market has marginal cumulative effects on the state of the system as a whole, it has a major impact on individual and organizational actors. The aggregative effects on the system are largely unnoticed, although from time to time the market may be used for particular political goals though withholding items from the market, boycotts, etc. Such actions have only short term consequences. With increased complexity of the market in terms of more and more variety of items, small changes in consumer or selling behavior begin to have political consequences, even planned ones. With future development, such uses of the markets for political goals become more and more frequent.

Participation in interaction systems accelerates the process of integration. Whereas production provides the properties for diversity and similarity, participation, or involvement, is a process that integrates diversity. First, in institutional participation there is inclusion of individuals into some participatory groups and organizations on the basis of their similarities with some and their differences with others. Second, along with increases in individual properties and increases in system diversity, more and more of the individual's properties become relevant to some part of the system, especially if his mobility increases. Thus, the extensiveness of the individual's ties to the system, through incorporation of more and more of his properties into structures that are increasingly differentiated, is increased. Third, because of the increasing number of both similarities and differences within the system, the strength of the individual's interdependence is increased. He becomes more dependent on the system. This dependency is manifest phenomenologically in social programs, in the use of the market to meet almost all needs, and, in general, in the lack of self-sufficiency. Dependence on the system strengthens the individual's ties to the system and is the basis for establishing his autonomy.

One salient characteristic of the individual's emerging in the system is that his variety is segmented. He is employee, family member, citizen, resident, consumer, and saver. These different roles are indicative of the fact that the variety of the individual is increasing but the system can deal with this only one property at a time. To the extent that these differences are compartmentalized and expressed in specialized institutions, they can be responded to. As these different roles become politicized over time, they become less and less separate spheres of activity for the individual and more and more part of his total personality.

Because development is a two fold function, that of similarities and differences, and because those differences which are central to participation and participatory institutions grow exponentially at some point, the system becomes out of touch with the existing diversity, as well as with the ways in which that diversity is becoming integrated. The system, for example, not only has to cope with mothers and workers but also with working mothers. Increases in diversity and variety and the integration of that variety at the individual level is one cause for the breakdown of the participatory institutions in interaction systems. Systems cannot change exponentially without undergoing basic transformations of their system function.

System Participation: Production in Transaction Systems

Since the dominant characteristic of transaction systems is flow of object properties and properties proper, there is no component intrinsic production—the activities of individuals or other components are almost entirely extrinsic. Productive activities are primarily fusion of properties proper and secondarily their diffusion. Each is exported to the system at large. Rather than specific components and networks, as is the case in interaction systems, properties proper are produced in the context of the total system and all of its complexity.

Production of properties proper thus takes place in the system as a whole. New ideas are the primary output. There must be intermediate organizations for production, since the system as a whole and the individuals within it are the producing units. Individuals rather than organizations or groups become the primary and dominant component of the system.

For properties proper there is no question of multiplication of the same item. Distribution takes place through diffusion, some components accepting and absorbing, others not. Individuals incorporate or fuse the ideas and select other ideas. The basis of social organization and of inclusion in the system is that of difference. Because differences are decisive in impacting the system, the number of redundant properties of similarity among components are reduced.

The assumption of upper limits still applies in that any component or any individual can have only so many different properties proper. An upper limit means that of the total variety of the system, the individual component will have a decreasing proportion of it. It also means that as the total variety of the system increases, the total number of properties proper that each individual will have approximates their upper limit and, thus, they will be nearly equal, depending on variation in the capacity of individuals. This near equality of properties proper, making each individual nearly equal in the number of properties, is the structural condition necessary for total inclusiveness, one of the dimensions of integration.

The assumption of upper limits and the continual increase in items of variety and their distribution into system diversity would mean that at a certain point the level of integrated diversity of the system itself would encounter an upper limit. Again, the upper limit of the system variety would be the upper limit of individual variety multiplied by the total number of individuals.

Several other processes at the component and system level, however, take place so that this upper limit to system variety is theoretically approached but never met. First, individuals can fuse two or more properties proper into one. An example of this would be a marine biologist who fuses knowledge from two fields. Rather than having two properties proper, he has one. In part, avoidance of the upper limit on individual variety is a motivational reason for fusion. Although fusions create new items of variety, they free the individual to acquire at least one additional property of variety. Second, an individual component can absorb only a small portion of the system's total properties proper and possesses it, but in effect, can have access to it, thus avoiding the upper limit. In transaction systems, characterized by flow and diffusion, if only one component has an item of variety, discounting for costs of access, every component of the system can have that property at some future point in time. What is required is locational information rather than actually having the property proper.[9] This locational information, furthermore, becomes organized through certain developmental processes, such as generalization. Third, there is a turnover of properties proper and a history of their turnover for each individual. Thus, a new item of variety can be acquired and another allowed to become dormant or transferred to some storage point in the system. Although there is an upper limit of the system, this limit applies only to a single point in time. New items of variety, both past and future, can continually be incorporated by the individual.

In transaction systems there are only two levels of system, the individual and the system as a whole. Various laws were used to explain this. The consequence is that the individual as a producing unit becomes enmeshed into or part of the system in which his productive activity is defined by his participation in that system.

Whereas in interaction systems the dominant mode of distribution is that of exchanges among specific components and sets of components, or within exchange networks (markets), in transaction systems the movement of properties proper throughout the physical and social space of the system is communication. Here the time cost distance functions that restrain exchange behavior are radically altered. First, although there are distance costs, the number of units in a given area (density) practically does not add cost per unit. Second, the cost per component receiving a property proper is nonlinear. The number of components receiving the message does not in any way affect the cost. Because of this, and Technology II previously discussed, there is almost total inclusiveness and a continual flow of properties proper.

Elaborate networks of communications allow information to flow at increasing rates. The elaboration of networks increases levels of integration among the individual components. Because messages are sent and received from the system at large, the individual becomes integrated with the system rather than linked to the system through intermediate structures and partial networks. The introduction of mass communication, indeed, destroys intermediate communication organizations and their hold on individuals. Whatever the level of complexity of a specific organization or group, the system as a whole, aggregating all the variety within the system, is able to provide more variety for the individual, better "quality" variety, and, thus, variety that is better suited to the individual's preferences than any subgroups. Properties proper that emanate from the system are, in short, superior to those emanating from any of its subsystems. Because of this, the individual gradually withdraws from subsystems and directs his behavior to the system at large.

The flow of properties proper from the system as a whole does not imply concentration or centralization. Indeed, because properties proper (some of which will take material form) are thoroughly dispersed, fusion, or production of properties proper, can take place anywhere in the system. These ideas are free, and as such, anyone can possess them. The free flow of properties is a precondition for the decline and dispersal of governmental power.

Component-System Relationships in the
Production of Properties Proper

Involvement of the component with the system involves three system-component linkages. First, there is the creation of properties proper through innovations, as well as productivity in innovations. Second, there are acts that disperse these properties through diffusion. Third, there are choices among alternatives that through communication aggregate into system level properties.

INNOVATION AND PRODUCTIVITY

Innovation is the creation of system level properties proper through the fusion of two or more properties proper or parts of them. The third, new property, is more than the sum of the two. Whereas in the combination of object properties, the whole can be deaggregated into its parts and the parts can be aggregated into the whole (at least in principle), a fusion of two or more properties proper is not deaggregative. Fusion takes place within the component or individual and the property that results is an integral part of it. Only some aspects of this new property can be encoded for diffusion throughout the system.

Productivity in transaction systems is a direct function of the total variety of properties proper that can be received by individuals. In the combination of object properties, the amount of variety that can be combined is limited.[10] For the fusion of properties proper, the probability of fusion is a direct function of the number and the total variety of the properties held or received. Productivity in transaction systems is system variety intensive rather than component capital intensive.

The shift from production to participation activities means that investment for productivity is in individual skills. Rather than investment in machinery, investments in individuals will be decisive. System level accumulation, as will be discussed, is defined in terms of providing everybody access to the total variety in the system.[11] Free, or unencumbered, access defines the wealth of the system rather than market value of identical properties.

The total variety of the system, as well as free access to every component of the system, determine individual productivity of properties proper. The producing organization is the system itself rather than any of its parts. Insofar as there is coordinated individual activity to produce variety, the main determinant of an individual's productivity is access to the system's variety of properties proper.

With an emphasis on producing variety through the participation of individuals, science becomes a productive rather than a supporting sector of other forms of production. Science, conceived broadly as organized search for variety and regularity, will become one of the dominant types of "production" that change the system. Continued increases in the variety of properties proper will depend on organized efforts to produce. Furthermore, the characteristics of organized scientific activity parallel those of transaction systems. They include (1) free flow of information and ideas; (2) temporary associations of individuals to bring together that variety which is essential to a particular kind of search; (3) status accorded to individually defined contributions with recognition of unique additions to the pool of properties proper; (4) clear identity of individual scientists with discoveries; and (5) the engagement of the total capacities of individual scientists, rather than their specific skills.

DIFFUSION

The second form of participatory activity in transaction systems concerns the transmittal of ideas throughout the system. Emphasis is given to expression. A major characteristic of transaction systems is the near total inclusion of individual components in networks of communication. Thus communication is with the system, which in effect means diffusion of communication throughout the entire system. Complete diffusion throughout the system is, of course, not possible because of the upper limits to variety. Properties proper are presented to the system, stored, and all components have more or less immediate access to all of the properties.

A basic problem in the transmission and flow of ideas is the distortion that inevitably follows encoding, transmitting, and decoding messages. Technology II stated that the time-cost-distance constraints on the movement of object properties would be continually reduced. For transaction systems, technology is assumed to diminish the distortions or noise in communication. Despite this, the exponential growth in diversity and variety from fusions of properties proper poses communication crises. Furthermore, the greater the density and complexity of the messages, the greater their distortion. To avert distortions that come from communicating with the system and to all components via the system, temporary social relationships and structures are formed for specific areas of communication.

In general, communication and the discovery of properties proper are merged. All individuals in highly developed transaction systems are both "scientists" or creators of properties proper and communicators. Although there are individual differences in terms of focal points of interest, creativity in expression is considered as much of a contribution as fusion of properties that underlie the content of what is communicated.

Full and free access to total system variety leads to an approximation of the full integration of the components into the system. The system "requires" every component or individual in order to translate its variety into diversity, although the proportion of total system properties held by the components declines. Again, all individuals thus tend to have an equal number of properties although a unique set of properties to the point of their upper limit.

Equality in numbers of properties meets the structural definition of equality in the system. What deviations from full equality that there are come from two sources. First, there are individual differences (although small) in capacity to absorb variety. Second, certain individuals have redundant variety, that is, duplicate the variety of other individuals. Variety that is redundant with that of others comes from not having full access to information about the system or not changing rapidly enough after information is received. The redundant variety of an individual constitutes a loss in the system's capacity to generate diversity. Even though information systems are improved to avoid losses from repetition of variety, there is always system slack.

ALTERNATIVES AND CHOICE

The third major way by which individuals can change the system is by instrumentally choosing certain courses of action in order to affect the state of the system. First, with increasing diversity within the system, the range of choices open to any individual is correspondingly increased. The number of alternatives continually increases. Second, any choice to involve oneself with the system, which properties to absorb, which to create, which to communicate, will have an impact on the nature of the system and its variety. These choices are not binding collective decisions. Binding decisions would per force emphasize some kinds of variety—a selection of similarity—at the expense of others. Individuals, rather, can act to provide the kind of societal environment they prefer, and the variety of the system will allow individuals to approximate their preferences. Thus, if there is no opportunity for a certain kind of activity, it is relatively easy for the individual to make or create such an activity and to communicate about it to others.

A salient characteristic of full participation in terms of choosing among alternatives and creating new ones is that every act is politicized or instrumental to some values and preferences. Decisions about what is consumed, whether or not to marry, whether or not to change residence will be perceived in terms of certain kinds of system outcomes that the individual considers desirable and preferable. The scope of activities that are involved in these political choices makes for almost complete extensiveness—all of the individual's properties being in some way tied to the system. This politicization is a type of full consciousness about the system and the individual's role in it.

Only highly integrated systems of great variety can, of course, absorb a high level of politicization without intense conflicts and instability. One characteristic of interaction systems is not only that they are unable to sustain high levels of politicization, but also that participation of one group is directed against other groups. One group allies or forms a coalition with others to oppose others. Governments are constantly called on to suppress conflicts in favor of dominant classes and groups. Politicization in transaction systems, however, is directed toward the system and changing it, rather than toward a particular part or segment of it. Thus, politicization does not generate conflict.

NOTES

1. Properties proper, of course, cannot be multiplied, only transformed or distributed.

2. For these kinds of systems, informants can provide a sound empirical basis for describing modalities of behavior. With differentiation, characteristic of interaction systems, sampling of variance is required, but central tendencies are appropriate descriptors. With almost total differences in transaction systems, normal distributions will give way to multimodal ones.

3. This preference was discussed in Chapter 2 in the context of the law of attractiveness of variety.

4. This discussion does not take into account monetarization, which is discussed later. The behavioral difference between barter and monetary economies is the direct or indirect nature of the exchange.

5. This assumption refers to the rate of total increase rather than per capita increase.

6. This is a general tendency for some levels of development. Since producing organizations are partially ecological and partially developmental, there are size constraints. Also, at high levels of development, large organizations will break up into smaller sized ones.

7. For most industrialized countries, most people were accorded individuality in the nineteenth century with registration of births and other forms of individual-governmental contact. With the gradual, sometimes sporadic, increases in individual differentiation, a few direct system-individual linkages were instituted, such as voting.

8. This involves the socialization of producing organizations through social ownership, worker control, or regulation.

9. Having or holding a property involves ownership, exclusion of others from its use. If access to a property is assured, then having a property becomes less relevant.

10. There is an exponential increase of effort required for a linear increase in the variety of object properties that are being combined.

11. One of the major qualitative differences between interaction and transaction systems is that in the former components can limit the access of others.

Chapter 5

THE DISTRIBUTION OF

SYSTEM PROPERTIES

For any level of development there are different patterns of distribution that are optimal for accelerating developmental change. Two systems with exactly the same number and kind of variety, the same number of total properties, and the same number of components can have two different structures of distribution, one leading to rapid and the other to relatively slow developmental change.

Distribution in Coaction Systems

In coaction systems, there are practically no distributive processes. There is, however, a theoretical distributional structure; it is a near identical possession of properties by every component. Each will have almost the same kind and number of properties and, thus, the properties of each component are generally redundant with those of every other component. This distribution of properties results in part from intrinsic production. Each component largely consumes what it produces. Because of this distribution there is little exchange.

Distribution in Interaction Systems

Exchange is a transfer of one object property for another across two or more components on the basis of some reciprocity. The principle of reciprocity means that for any object property sent another is received, directly or indirectly. Interaction systems are often characterized by transfers with little reciprocity. Object properties are unequally distributed, limited both in number and by ownership. Thus there is competition, exploitation, and overt conflict.[1]

A decisive distinction between coaction and interaction systems that have some elements of exchange is that there is some diversity. At low levels of development in interaction systems, diversity comes primarily from redundant identities. Some types of distributional structures are based on redundant identities.[2]

One feature of interaction systems with little diversity is that exchanges of particular object properties will tend to result in stratification, based on redundant properties. Thus, that component which has more redundancy can change one or more properties with another component with less redundancy. The consequence, however, will be only a change in the distribution of properties rather than greater equality among components. Thus, without force or means other than exchange, or without an expansion in the number of properties, asymmetrical relationships can remain unchanged, even if there is "exchange."

Relative power relationships follow from the distribution of properties. In general, those components with the most redundant object properties will be dominant. It is the pattern of sharing and accumulation of properties that defines the nature of the social structure and the relationships among the components.

The structure of the distribution that follows processes of exchange depends on a number of factors, such as the level and rate of production, but especially on the overall level of development of the system. Exchanges lead to development if the transfer of object properties from one component to another increases the diversity of the system, and if that transfer leads to combinations producing a new item of variety or to an increase in the number of the identical object properties. The first adds diversity, the second variety.

DISTRIBUTION AND PRODUCTION

At higher levels of development, when exchanges are resulting in a continuous growth of diversity, productive processes become linked to distributive ones. Once this linkage, at first weak, is effected, development proceeds. Production affects the nature of distribution, which affects consumption and accumulation, which in turn affects production.

Several developmental conditions are required before this production-distribution function emerges. First, there must be some distribution of properties such that transfers will increase, at least initially, both the similarities and variety of the components, without reducing the total variety or diversity of the system. There must be something to be exchanged, even if only redundant identities. Second, there must be a number of components involved in exchange sufficient for "substantial" component extrinsic production. There must be sufficient demand for a specific level of distribution to function as a stimulus to production. Third, there must be enough absortive capacity to accumulate the items that are being produced, thus increasing the system's diversity.

This production-distribution relationship is twofold. What is produced affects how it is distributed and the distribution affects what is produced. This leads to two possible patterns of the development of interaction systems at low levels of diversity. The first is to combine abundant identities into a new item of variety and to make that item of variety also abundant. This would be a pattern of widespread distribution but little system diversity, often leading to relatively low levels of productivity and underutilization of the existing variety by making it unavailable to organized productive processes. Integration through similarities would dominate interaction through diversity. The second pattern is to use most existing variety to produce new items, and these new items are utilized for production. Variety is immediately taken into the productive processes. This pattern would lead to underutilization of similarity for development but more rapid increases in variety. The first of these would emphasize distributive equality; the second, expanding diversity and inequality. Both of these patterns have limits points where development stops.

EXCHANGE AND INEQUALITY

Exchange processes are based on asymmetrical distribution of properties. The general theoretical premise is that the greater the similarity and differences among two components, the greater the probability of an act of exchange. But to the extent that diversity is based on a limited number of properties unequally distributed, there is a tendency for those components with the greatest variety to accumulate the properties, impoverish the variety of other components and, thus, reduce the total amount of system diversity. With reduction in diversity following an increase in the total number of properties, there can be, if other factors do not intervene, a decline in the rate of development.[3]

Concentration in interaction systems can lead to rapid increases in the production of variety. In general, the greater the level of development the greater the variety required by components in order to produce additional items of variety. In relatively low developed interaction systems, the concentration of a few properties of some variety is sufficient for a combination of properties. Since the total variety of the system is increasing at an accelerating rate, the new properties that have been recently produced and that are available in limited quantities if concentrated are more likely to be used to produce a new item than if they were distributed. The rate of producing variety will exceed that of producing identities at some intermediate level of development of interaction systems. This will mean that newly produced variety that is limited in quantity tends toward concentration, and this concentration makes probable additional new properties which are again initially concentrated. In part, concentration results from the law of attractiveness of variety: the components with high levels of variety attract those components with the most variety. Those with less variety attract less variety. Over time, the transformation of items of variety into items of similarity reduces concentration.

Increasing exchange depends on reducing the asymmetry of relationships among components and increasing the number of properities of all components in order to increase the potential for reciprocity. Only under conditions of reciprocity can exchanges enhance the probability of variety in the components. Without reciprocity, the total of diversity of the system will be reduced by a tendency to concentrate.

As development increases, an increasing proportion of total exchanges takes place among organizations, institutions, and groups. Variety is accumulated by institutions and the greatest amount of variety by those institutions which produce the most variety—those of size and complexity which have certain strategic positions in the system. Individuals as independent components of the system do not emerge as actors until they have some accumulation of similarities and differences. When they begin to do so, they at first will have an impact largely through mass aggregations of atomized individual decisions, such as those in the market.

As individuals become the major actors in the system and as they acquire sufficient numbers and variety of properties, reciprocity in exchanges and equality among individuals will increase. A relative level of equality is a precondition for the transformation of an interaction system into a transaction system where the flow of properties takes place without consideration of the actual distribution of properties among components. Furthermore, the extent to which there are segments of the population that are not included in the system (low inclusiveness) by virtue of their lack of properties, will be the extent to which the emergence of characteristics of transaction systems will be mixed and slow. In other words, the extent to which each individual can participate in the interaction system on the basis of reciprocity is the extent to which the system will move to transactions and away from exchanges.

EXCHANGE AND CONFLICT

One of the consequences of the distribution of properties in interaction systems is cleavages and conflicts. Cleavage is defined by discontinuities in similarities linking components, however indirectly. Thus, if two components share a property which is not shared by the third, there is a cleavage. Despite the structure of discontinuities, what is of interest for exchange is the extent to which discontinuities in similarities preclude exchange and, thus, components acquiring properties. Cleavages then, in terms of this theory, can be defined formally as discontinuities in similarities or breaks in the linkages of similarities in a social system. The probability of exchanges across cleavages is low.

This distribution of properties also defines the conditions for conflict within the system. Conflict structures are distributions of properties, such that it is almost impossible for one or more component to obtain properties in exchange. The concentration of properties inhibits their movement to certain components. Thus, the distribution of properties with some development leads to a range of conditions of competition. Some components obtain properties and are "better off." Others do not have either a sufficient number or variety of properties to engage in exchange and have no opportunity of becoming "better off." Because, at least at low levels of exchange, the distribution of properties is asymmetrical, and tends to lead to the accumulation of variety in a few components, objective conditions of conflict are present.[4]

Actual conflict behavior, however, requires both subjective and objective explanatory factors. The subjective conditions necessary for conflict behavior occur when the objective conditions are present, excluding misperception or irrational behavior. In this theory, the dynamics by which these objective conditions are translated into subjective factors which lead to conflict behavior are not taken into account. The objective conditions, which are a necessary but not sufficient cause of conflict behavior, are, however, directly derivable from the theory—that is, from the total number of properties in a system, the variety, the diversity, the similarities, and the dominant distributive processes.

Distribution in Transaction Systems

The basic underlying characteristic of transaction systems is the flow of properties proper. The distributive processes shift from exchanges among components to the reception and transmission of properties proper to and from the system. Furthermore, the emphasis, as it is to a limited extent in interaction systems, is on having access to variety rather than having variety. Having access to variety is the way an individual can manage to have a substantial amount of variety, given the abundance of available variety and the unlimited possibilities to be unique.

The distributive process of transaction systems tends to be universal. Distinctiveness through the accumulation of properties is unlikely.

Even if other individuals have the same property, it is highly improbable that they will have it in the same combination or set as any other individual. Thus, two individuals may know the same things, but what they can do with what they know will be different.

The use of properties proper, such as a skill, enhances rather than detracts from its value. Furthermore, the acquisition of properties proper does not preclude anyone else from having it, as is the case for object properties. Indeed, any property proper is by definition available in abundance, equal in "number" to the total number of components of the system. The only restriction on the "abundance" of the property for the system is that there are a limited number of components and a limited component capacity to absorb them.

As an interaction system approaches transformation into a transaction system, there is near universalization of reciprocity in exchanges. Object properties as a source of diversity diminish in comparison to properties proper. Changes in the nature of object properties shift to those of quality, particularly product integration, but these qualitative differences become increasingly marginal.

Achievement of full reciprocity of relationships diminishes the role of exchange as a means of controlling scarcity. Once there is full reciprocity, which means an equal capacity of individuals to claim the properties that they desire, institutional mechanisms of control, such as accounting, become less necessary. Indeed, with reciprocity and relative abundance because of the shift of production from object properties to properties proper, traditional symbols of exchange—money, record keeping, and the like—are replaced by a generalized rights to claim. This shift from specific claims deriving from accumulation to a generalized right to claim first takes place in areas of properties proper, primarily in the service sectors, such as education and health. These sectors are the first to move out of exchange structures to the modalities of transaction systems. This occurs in part because the distribution of properties proper can be organized to increase efficiencies in diffusion. Such distributions can be achieved through distribution centers rather than through decentralized exchange points. Again, what is decisive for individuals is access to system services, or properties proper, when wanted or needed.

Rights to claim tend to be increasingly general, become detached from specific forms of behavior, and are extended in time.[5] This frees individuals from control over their behavior, which is characteristic of interaction systems, leading to more individual autonomy. These claims derive from system membership and are not to be tied to either instrumental behavior or reciprocity.

Beginning in interaction systems and dominating transaction systems is the transfer of properties proper to the system or to points in the system where they can be assessed. Elimination of barriers to access reduces the necessity for possession. What is diffused is information about the location of properties in the system. In interaction systems object properties are located within the market rather than being possessed by the components, even in areas of "vital" importance, such as food. In the case of information about what is known and what can be predicted from what is known, this information is initially in understandardized form necessitating face-to-face contact in large agglomerations, such as cities, in order to locate and interpret information for prediction. Only when information is standardized can it be dispersed to a large number of locations. Lack of standardization can be overcome by direct communication which presents information in a context that can be understood.

In interaction systems, distribution becomes increasingly tied to production. In transformation systems the productive processes become detached from the processes of distribution and are "market insensitive." There are two reasons for this detachment. First, the absorptive capacity for variety of highly developed systems means that almost any kind of variety, even if it is different from existing variety only by fancy, can be, at least for some time, absorbed by the system. Almost any new idea in transaction systems has some reception, fitting somewhere. Second, with the flow of properties proper the production of properties occurs without regard to the process of distribution. The "idea" is registered with the system and its diffusion does not exclude any components.

Distribution in transaction systems follows from the free diffusion of properties proper, limited by resources which are exogeneous to this theory. This means that there is near equality in the number and variety of properties up to the limit of individual capacity. Furthermore, properties proper are cheaply available because once a property proper is put together, or fused, and entered into the system, that property has been produced once and for all, for all components. Its distribution is constrained only by small and diminishing costs of diffusion. The availability of properties proper to all components sharply contrast them with the multiplication in production of object properties to approximately one for every one through mass production. Because of the accelerating rate of producing properties proper, there is an almost unlimited number of different properties for components to choose from and to discard. It is possible, therefore, for an individual to change the composition of his variety almost continuously.

This relatively full equality, at least with regard to those properties proper which will be more highly valued in transaction systems rather than object properties, means that the objective conditions for conflict diminish. The demands for coercion to rectify inequalities that occur in the distribution of object properties, resulting from development, are no longer present. With equality the system is able to achieve its maximum diversity and rate of development.

Accumulation

Accumulation affects both the rate of production of properties in the system and their integration. What is accumulated is a function of what is produced and consumed both by the system and by the components.

Accumulation directly affects the amount of similarity and diversity of the system. In interaction systems any accumulation of a property by a component is for the system tantamount to the consumption of that property. The property is taken out of the process of distribution. Accumulation is, however, a precondition for production by components, for only with some level and kind of accumulation is it possible for the component to produce additional object properties. It is in the context of production that accumulation is a social process basic to development.

UNITS THAT ACCUMULATE

In coaction systems, the only accumulating unit is the component. In interaction systems, accumulation occurs in organizations, in individuals, and, to an increasing extent, in the system itself. The shift from individuals to organizations as units of accumulation means the individual's dependence on other components and, to some extent, on the system itself. In transaction systems, the primary point of accumulation is the system as a whole. What is important for the individual is the fact that he has access to properties. But because of the rate of the flow of properties in the system, the number of properties actually accumulated by individuals declines as a proportion of the total. Accumulation in transaction systems becomes detached from the dynamics of developmental change.

PRODUCTION AND ACCUMULATION

In interaction systems accumulation is investment if one of two consequences follow: accumualtion is a necessary condition for the production of a new item of variety or accumulation leads to increases in productivity of identical properties. Accumulation-productive functions in transaction systems contrast with those of interaction systems in that the basic accumulating unit is the system itself rather than the components and the system. Each component has access to what is accumulated. This access means, for example, that accumulations of properties are "subsidized" by the system and that no organization within the system is able to match the accumulated properties of the system. Because the production of properties proper is variety intensive, and the variety intensity is rapidly increasing in comparison to the last item of variety produced, new properties will reflect substantial increments over the variety required for the last new property. This exponential increase in the variety needed for new variety cannot be provided by any set of system components.

Highly developed interaction systems reflect the logic that new items of greater complexity require organizations of greater scale capable of accumulating greater variety. The complexity of the last new item of variety produced may exceed the capacity of the organization for producing another item of still greater complexity.

Those sectors where there is a push toward ever increasing variety begin to take on the characteristics of transaction systems. This push explains the high level of integration of some levels of components in interaction systems.

ABSORPTIVE CAPACITY

Absorptive capacity of a system is the ability of the components and of the system itself to take on or possess a property. It can be assessed by the probability of the components or the system receiving additional properties. The absorptive capacity of interaction systems decreases as a function of the number of properties and the variety that the component or system has. The absorptive capacity of transaction systems is practically unlimited.

Absorptive capacity determines how components and the system respond to increasing variety. In coaction systems there are almost no items of component variety. The system is dominated by identities, and accumulation is not inhibited by increases in quantity except by certain "environmental" constraints, such as land. In interaction systems, variety and identities are for the most part possessed by the components, and some components have substantially more than others. This variety of the components shift to subsystems with higher levels of variety which are among the first to become directly enmeshed into the system. In transaction systems, the amount of variety available continues to expand exponentially, enabling the individual to be unique, and continue to be so, by continually restructuring his variety, being a different "person" each day. Furthermore, the rate of producing new items of variety depends on absorbing the most recent properties, those that have just been created. The new properties will generally incorporate all of the relevant variety in a particular domain. The process of development is dependent on absorbing and transforming the variety contained in new properties.

Absorption is of two basic kinds. First, components can organize their properties and the absorption of any additional properties will be influenced by the structure of the existing properties. Second, there is simple aggregation of additional properties without regard to what kind they are—each has, in effect, its own place and is independent of the others. The first of these is more characteristic of properties proper, generally information rather than "data." The second, is more characteristic of object properties. Either type, however, can either be organized or simply aggregated. In general, the greater the variety available in the system, the greater the tendency for the components to organize rather than aggregate properties in order to acquire the additional available variety. The organization of properties, both item object and properties proper, is critical for development, since it is the foundation of the process of rationalization, which will be discussed.

The greater the degree of organization of properties by a component, the greater the probability that accumulating properties will lead to a combination or fusion, the creation of a new property. Thus, the higher the level of development, the greater the variety; the greater the availability of variety, the greater the propensity of components to select and organize properties; the greater the selectivity, the higher will be the probability that a component will create still a new item of variety.[6] In this way, the processes of accumulation contributes to accelerating the rate of development.

With development the combined object properties and the fused properties proper will themselves be of greater and greater complexity. The cumulative effects of development will be in those domains with the greatest variety. Thus, any new property produced could reflect all, or a substantial part of all previous variety in that area. For example, some new idea can be the fusion of all previous ones in the area plus one additional element and, thus, will supercede all previous ideas.

LIMITS TO ABSORPTION

The basic problem for highly developed interaction systems and their components with the greatest variety, as well as for transaction system, is how to absorb exponentially increasing variety. One conclusion, of course, is that saturation and further development will stop, following a sine curve, used to describe the growth of proportions.[7] This issue arises from the theoretical implication that at any point in time it is possible to calculate a theoretical upper limit of variety for components, the total diversity of the system which is the product of all components, and the upper limit of variety for each component. This does not include the total variety that can be absorbed by the system, which can store considerably more variety than is in use by the components. But only that variety in use at any point in time can be expected to be productive of new items of variety.

With development and continually expanding variety, the following patterns allow the components to absorb, and thus use, the existing variety of the system. First, an increasing proportion of total variety is stored in the system, and there is increasingly efficient access to that variety, which is assumed to follow from Technology II, the reduction in time-cost-distance restraints. Increasingly more variety will be available than actually is used. Second, the rate of discarding properties increases. Items become "obsolete." That which is discarded can be stored for some future use. Whether discarded or stored, the property in effect is taken out of the flow of properties that can be used for production or participation. Each involves some loss, either through "noise" in the storage process or from depletion.

The fundamental question for continued development at very high levels of development is how can variety be kept in use without component and system overload. Overload can be avoided by retaining the variety without holding the properties manifesting that variety. This is achieved in two ways. First, the properties are combined or fused into something new, and for the most part what was characteristic of what was combined or fused is retained in the new object property or property proper, discounting for some loss in the process. Instead of two properties there is one. The loss in the capacity of the component to hold variety has been reduced. This "reduction" in the properties of the component does not reduce the complexity of the properties of the component. The second way is exchanging or discarding several items of variety for a unit of complexity that substitutes for the previous variety. Variety is thus integrated into the complexity of a property at the component level and this property, incorporating complexity, becomes only one item rather than many. Properties themselves, thus, absorb variety.

The system's ability to store properties is directly related to how much the components have absorbed. Components can themselves store properties for accessing by other components. To the extent that the system can store an item so that it can be accessed with the least amount of information by other components, access to the most information with the least information, is the extent to which the system can increase its absorptive capacity. For object properties the system can provide not only information about the location of the object property in time and space, but also how quickly the component can actually obtain it and at what "cost." This latter is important since, in general, access to an object property means possession at some future point in time and involves, therefore, movement and its time-cost distance constraints.

ABSORPTIVE MECHANISMS

There are several absorptive mechanisms in the system depending on its level of development and the types of properties involved. In interaction systems these mechanisms are largely institutions—government, libraries, and research institutes. Information about what is stored and how to access it increasingly becomes one of the most critical "commodities" of interaction systems. Reducing costs of access is directly related to the processes of standardization and rationalization. Indeed, the storage capacity of both the components and the system is a primary explanatory factor of development.

For transaction systems a high proportion of the total variety of the components is in a state of flow, that is, "in" the communication networks. The primary mechanism for the absorption and storage of properties proper are information systems about the variety of all components. The networks of communication will be the primary form of organizing the absorption of the variety that exists in components. In addition, there are technological mechanisms that can provide information about all previous variety in the form of accessible records. These will be located at places in the system devoted to recording, storing, and providing access to variety that is not stored by components. In general, the tendency for systems beginning to become transaction systems is the increasing "value" of information about the location of variety. Information about variety will generally be only slightly less "valued" than actually "having" the variety.

ABSORPTION AND INTEGRATION

As the properties of a component become integrated, the rate at which new properties (a new item of variety) will be integrated will increase. The more a component is integrated into the system the greater the probability that any property that is created by that component will be absorbed by the system. In part this is because variety that is added to systems with high levels of integrated diversity is proportionally less than the total variety added; and the lower the proportion, the less the reduction in the system's integration.

With respect to inclusion and extensiveness, if only a few properties of a component are linked to the system and if the component does not share properties with other components or similarities, then adding new variety to that component will compound the differences among the components and contribute to cleavages. The absorption of variety by the system thus depends on "who" acquires that variety. If it is a component that is weakly integrated, the additional variety will weaken the level of integration of the system even more. If the component is well integrated, the additional variety will be readily absorbed, as this additional variety requires relatively little integrative "effort."

In empirical systems there are differences between the actual level of variety of the components and the absorptive capacity of the system for variety. Less developed systems will have difficulty absorbing the variety of some components (many of which will have taken on their variety from outside of the system). In such situations there might be conscious collective action to suppress variety or remove the component from the system, or alternatively, for those components with great variety to change the system. When the level of development is high and accelerating, there is almost no possibility that any component will have variety equal to the system, and any kind of variety can be readily absorbed.

The relationships between development, the total amount of diversity, and the absorptive capacity of the system can be explained in terms of what is structurally deviant. What differences are responded to as deviant depends on the actual range of differences within the system. If the distribution of a property is relatively peaked rather than "normal," indicating a high level of conformity, any slight absolute movements will depart from the range of differences. If the range of differences is wide, however, an equal increase in differences will be less likely to deviate from the range of the population. Furthermore, the probability of absorbing "deviant" properties, or a deviant component, into the system is directly related to their closeness to other properties or components.

Consumption

Consumption either decomposes a property or depletes it in some way. The consequence of consumption in a particular unit of time is to reduce the total number of properties in the system.

There is a fundamental difference between consumption of an item object property, a "material good," and "consumption" of a property proper. The consumption of an object property reduces the total number of properties in the system and, if that property contributed to diversity, the total diversity of the system. This reduction, however, must be adjusted for the rate of production of identical object properties.

Consumption will reduce the total diversity and similarity of the system if the rate of consumption is faster than the rate of production, or if the relative rates of consumption of components results in a change in the distribution of properties that lessen similarity and diversity. Patterns of consumption and the structure of distribution are linked. If the distributive processes are linked in such a way that consumption leads to a reduction in the total number of properties, and in the similarity and diversity of the system, the function of consumption in development is negative. The condition of a slow or negative rate of development is either that the consumption of items is in some state of balance with production, which depends on the distributive processes, leading to stagnation, or that the rate of consumption exceeds the rate of production, leading to retrogression—losing both similarities and differences of production.

Systems that are near the point of an exponential rate of development often have highly fluctuating rates of consumption and production. How frequent and large these fluctuations will be depends on the relationships among consumption, distribution, and accumulation. If the distribution of object properties is weighted in favor of high consuming units rather than accumulating units, then the production of new properties and redundant similarities will slow. Whether or not this happens depends on whether several processes of accumulation have a positive effect on production and productivity.

At high levels of development the impact of distributive processes on patterns of consumption diminishes. At low levels of development, consumption generally depresses the rate of production. However, at higher levels of development, when the capacity of the system for production is high, consumption may be a positive factor in development. Once a particular object property is fully distributed and the diversity that can be derived from the distribution of redundant identities has passed the point of diminishing differences, the stimuli to continued production are consumption and decay. At this point, however, the replacement of similarity and diversity has little impact on the rate of developmental change but it maintains a particular level of development. The object property becomes marginal, less valued for its contribution to distinctiveness.

The "consumption" of properties proper involves neither decomposition nor depletion. Rather than consumption there is use or nonuse of the property. The property proper can be more or less effectively utilized for developmental change: it cannot be consumed. Thus the impact that a property proper has on similarity or diversity remains for all time, until it becomes obsolete because of its incorporation into another property proper of greater complexity. This is a major reason that the rate of developmental change becomes exponential in highly developed systems. The variety of the system becomes equal to the potential total similarity among all components.

Properties proper are free from consumption restraints. Their potential contributions to development are lost to the system in terms of development only by the costs of access or restrictions on those who could use them to produce new variety. The logical consequence of these theoretical arguments, especially if technology is continually improved, is a point where there is comprehensive and instantaneous access—a theoretical point, never to be fully achieved.

Decay

Decay has an impact on development similar to consumption. Decay differs from consumption in that it is largely independent of distribution. It has two basic forms: there is natural decay from physical forces that results in decomposition and depletion, and there is social decay that results in the tendency of all systems, especially social ones, to run down over time.

Natural decay can be defined as the life of an object property not in social use. In some cases, social use may slow down the rate of decay, but this is only a short term effect. The rate of social use decay varies with the level of development of the system and complexity of the object properties. The greater the complexity of object properties (the number of different object properties that are combined to produce a new item object), the greater the social use decay, but this is offset by greater complexity and integration of the property. The social usefulness of less integrated objects declines, however, with development. In general, the higher the level of development, the greater the tolerances required for an object property to be integrated into the system.

Although there is no natural decay of properties proper, the law of negative entropy applies. The greater the variety that is fused into the property proper, the greater tendency of social use decay. Also the greater the information contained in the property, the greater the absolute loss of information. What is lost is a direct function of what is available, the loss as a proportion of all that is present continually declines as the complexity of the properties proper increases.

All systems are subject to the law of negative entropy including developmental systems. What is important is the rate of entropy in comparison to the rate of development. By definition the entropy of the total system must be less than its rate of development. For highly developed systems, highly integrated systems, it is appropriate to speak of the rate of decay of the system as a whole. For less integrated systems, the law of negative entropy applies more appropriately to sectors of the system. The greater the complexity of that sector, the greater is its entropy.

Obsolescence applies to both object properties and properties proper. Obsolescence is defined as points in time where a new object property proper comes to the fore which incorporates all of the variety of a previous property and at least one additional item of variety (a change in quality). When this is the case, the previous item will be superseded and will be obsolete. For example, a machine that does everything another does and does so with less cost or with one other function, such as inspection, makes others obsolete. Because the rate of the production of variety increases with development, the rate of obsolescence also increases accordingly. Development and obsolescence are thus directly related.

The accelerating rate of obsolescence poses the problem of discarding properties. Decay can be a positive factor in development, both in its social and natural forms, by removing properties and thereby allowing the components and the system to take on new ones of higher complexity. As development increases, the rate of decay will be too slow in comparison to the rate at which new properties appear. The problem then, is one of consciously acting to accelerate decay of object properties in order to free the system to increase its level of development. The "discard" problem for properties proper is only one of storage.

NOTES

1. Many such "coercive" transfer payments, "grant economy" transactions, can be interpreted as economic payments in exchange for political neutrality or support.

2. One such is a "perfect" hierarchy. For example, if there are ten items of variety and ten properties of each item, it is possible to distribute these properties in a hierarchical pattern of frequency, that is, several properties to one individual, one less to to another, etc.

3. Governmental transfers can, of course, offset the decline of development resulting from overaccumulation of some components. Some redistribution under these circumstances would stimulate development by increasing the systems potential for exchange.

4. Conflicts are intensified within systems when those components with the most variety and properties trade with other systems for additional properties. Such an alternative, of course, requires open systems. The combination of development and openness will stimulate governmental intervention.

5. For example, earning will be defined in terms of months, years, and even a lifetime rather than hours, days or weeks.

6. These processes are exemplified in the contrast between the more developed theoretical sciences where each new idea builds on previous knowledge, some totally superseding the old or replacing it in comparison to descriptive sciences where each new item

is put along side others, having no impact on the others, except to increase aggregatively the scope of knowledge.

7. The sine curve expresses slow proportional growth at the beginning then a rapid increase, followed by a tapering off as the proportion reaches 1.00. Such a curve, however, often observed for specific phenomena, such as the growth of publications in a science, is partly an artifact of the definition of proportion.

PART III

DEVELOPMENTAL PROCESSES AND

MANIFESTATIONS

Development and developmental change as defined in this general theory have almost an unlimited range of historical manifestations. This part deals with a few general ones.

Chapter 6 discusses the characteristics of the structures of the social system that are perceptible, contained in an information system about the social system.

Chapter 7 is only a general introduction to the empirical study of development. It deals with four kinds of developmental manifestations—socialization and individualization, differentiation and specialization, equality and inequality, and conflict and cooperation.

Chapter 6

COGNITIVE PROCESSES

Although diversity is an objective property of a system, integration involves behavior, and thus must be linked in some way to cognition. Although cognition assumes individual and organizational responses, what will be discussed here are observable properties of structures and the relationships among structures which are manifest. These cognitive aspects of structure can be considered both manifest and latent, the latter being characteristics of the social structure that are not explicitly and consciously "recognized" by individuals or groups.

Integrated diversity or development cannot be seen in the common sense meaning of "see." It must be inferred from sets of observations and put together with complex composition rules that have been described. In the same sense other structural properties cannot be seen but must be inferred from observations of individuals, of their behavior, and of physical objects, including their spatial and temporal relationships. Structural properties, however, manifest themselves in a variety of ways which involve cognitive processes of developmental change.

The Symbolic Content of Structure

Properties of the social structure are translated into characteristics of behavioral relevance to individuals, groups, and organizations through symbolic content. This symbolic content becomes the behavioral "stimuli," which facilitate or inhibit integrative processes, thereby affecting development. The relationships between structural changes and their symbolic manifestations in developmental systems are such that the interactions and transactions result in increased interdependence. Properties of structures that facilitate development are relational properties among components, such as standardization.

Symbols both reflect the social structure and influence it. Of course, the symbol system of a society, expressed in its language, its myths, its art, reflects more than social structure. Furthermore, of the total amount and kind of recognized differences in symbols, only a part is behaviorally relevant. The symbols of the social system are, nevertheless, the critical link between "reality" and behavior. The focus of this discussion is the symbol system as "reality" or meaning rather than its relevance to behavior.

In coaction systems what is important is the functions of symbols rather than their content. These symbol systems in mythology, religion, and witchcraft have very similar integrative functions or "meaning" for such types of societies, even with wide variety in actual content.[1] The important functions of the symbols are to express similarity and reinforce existing relationships in terms of common origins and a common fate. Also, because of the high dependence of coaction societies on the physical environment, much of the symbolic representation is of salient environmental factors, such as rain, crops, and good hunting.

In developmental systems, however, the content of the symbols, and not just their functions, takes on meaning in terms of developmental change. In interaction systems what is important are representations of object properties. Of all characteristics of object properties, the degree to which they are expressed in standard units, arbitrarily chosen units of measurement, becomes decisive in terms of the ways in which one object located at one point in physical and social space can be related to others. Standardization is, however, only one such relational property of significance for developmental change. Universalization of the standard units, that is, the commonality of the units, also becomes decisive in reducing the costs of interaction and in facilitating combinations of object properties. Historically, the critical symbolic expression of object properties was money, and later, the international monetary system.

In contrast to coaction systems the distinguishing characteristic of symbols in developmental systems is their correspondence to social reality. With such correspondences it is possible to exchange object properties and to enter properties proper into the system. The symbol system becomes, although arbitrary in form, nonarbitrary in content. Thus a "measure" of a unit reflects a "real" property of a unit, and to the extent that the measure is in stand-and units, each such unit can relate and be related to every other unit. Such cognitively "real" properties make it possible for systems to extend beyond random encounters for exchange or beyond a particular setting for receiving and sending ideas. The cognitive content thus becomes the foundation for conscious activities leading to development.

Although correspondence is important, the character of the content is also decisive. This involves a difference between the cognitive representation of experience and the symbolic structuring of information. The more variety a particular symbol expresses, the greater its potential importance in facilitating the integration of diversity.

There are substantial incongruities between structural realities and their symbolic representation. Such differences will vary with the level of development. These incongruities can be either that the cognitive structure reflects more diversity and similarity than actually is the case or that it reflects less. Although a number of hypotheses could be generated concerning this incongruity, one general one is that the more rapid the development, the less proportionally the symbol system will reflect changes in diversity and the more proportionally, therefore, it will reflect similarities. Another such hypothesis concerns the willful creation of symbols that reflect more development than is the case in order to stimulate diversity or integration. Symbolic representation can emphasize similarity in the face of diversity or diversity in the face of similarity. In general, the lower the level of development, the higher will be the incongruity between symbols and "reality."

Rationalization

Rationalization is the primary linkage between social structure and social symbols. It involves cognitive mapping in which relationships among components and their properties are expressed. Rationalization is a property of the symbols of a social system. A symbol system is more rationalized to the extent that it is inclusive of the diversity and to the extent that it corresponds with reality of the social system. Rationalization is the basic elaboration of the cognitive structure that expresses more aspects of the social structure more accurately.

Another way of expressing the "reality" dimension of rationalization is secularization, a concept that is usually counterposed with the "sacred." Sacred symbols, although they have complex characteristics, are generally extramundane, that is, they have no direct linkage to empirical reality, and are unchanging, not reflecting changes in society or the physical environment. Another characteristic of sacred symbols is that they are exclusive, referring to specific sets of "things" in a specific setting. The inclusiveness dimension of rationalization is in opposition to the sacred character of symbols. Although secularization may be seen as a developmental process in terms of cognitive properties of developmental processes, it directly follows from the definition of rationalization.

One of the differences between symbol systems characterized by rationalization and those by little or none of it is whether or not the symbol systems take on lives of their own. Once this happens, there is a divergence between the reality of a social system and the behavior of its individual components. Behavior, rather than being linked to the social structure and its changes through a symbol system, becomes tied to the symbol system itself. Thus what is believed about social reality becomes the predictor of behavior. Such systems may indeed relate their social behavior almost entirely to a mythology or religion. Rationalized social systems must, however, make continuous corrections in their symbol system to correspond with the actual social structure.

Standardization

Standardization refers to the logical languages in which properties proper and object properties are expressed. To the degree that the "units" or measures of such properties are expressed in stand-are, or known units, usually uniform and equal units, each "unit" can be compared. Thus information about a property of any component can be compared with that about the same property of all other units.

Units of comparison usually arise for specific classes of objects. The most general and familiar of these are size and weight. Standards for specific areas become generalized by their uniformity and by their multidimensionality. Additional properties of objects or components become standardized after some of the basic properties have become standardized. For object properties, the most important basic characteristic is physical displacement. Additional types of properties that gradually become standardized include the life of an object, its color, and lumination. For properties proper, skills in terms of performance become standardized, such as performance expectations of education or trades.

Although uniform units are often the most simple to use for comparisons, what is important in standardization is not the uniform nature of the units but rather their translatability from one language of measurement into another. Uniformity in the application of arbitrary measurement languages obviates the need for such translation rules. The critical questions for standardization are, however, the rules for moving from one measurement language into another, and the ease of deriving comparisons among properties.

Standardization does not generate uniformity of properties but, rather, is the foundation for combining and fusing properties to create new variety and diversity. To the extent that properties are standardized, properties of different objects can be combined or fused. The initial role of standardization is to provide for increased combinatorial capacity through a reduction in differences among properties. Thus, there are slight reductions in differences in degree but substantial increases in combinatorial possibilities. Not only do similar properties of different components become interchangeable, but also different properties of different components.

Standardization also refers to categories which are uniform. A standard category means that any object labelled as a member of a particular category would have a predictable set of properties.

The greater the number of properties that are indicated by a particular category, the more information the label conveys, but at the cost of accuracy in terms of discrimination. In this sense standardization simplifies differences by grouping, conveying information of a general sort but obscuring information of particular kinds.

The major implication of standardization for developmental change concerns the ease of exchanging and transferring properties. As a result of standardization, the range of component search for properties can expand and information about available properties allows greater selectivity. Standardization and comparisons of units is the basis for calculating comparative advantages of exchange.

Generalization

Although the concepts of generalization and discrimination are taken from psychology, they are used here to refer to characteristics of the symbol system that reflect social reality. The cognitive domain can be considered as potential stimuli which have partial correspondences with reality and which actually stimulate behavior.

The process of generalization and discrimination closely parallels that of integrating diversity. The diversity or new variety becomes cognitively differentiated by smaller and smaller margins. But, at the same time, discrimination or labelling of increasingly smaller differences occurs in the context of a structure that allows for more and more variety to be expressed in fewer and fewer hierarchically ordered symbols. Thus there is both increased symbolic recognition of differences and increased organization of these differences through generalization-indicating commonalities. The commonalities enable object properties and properties proper to be connected in time and space.

This dual process of generalization and discrimination takes place after some level of diversity has been attained. Diversity is the basis for generalization, once that diversity becomes identifiable. Generalization is, in other words, generated by variation. But discrimination also requires generalization in that one property or one object has to be seen as different from another. In this sense the symbolic system expresses the similarities and differences in the system: the greater the generalization or expressed similarities, the greater the expressed diversity. Knowing that something is different requires knowing that it is similar. The process is iterative: one emanates from the other.

There are various characteristics of generalized symbols in addition to that of "correspondence" already mentioned. First, there is discrimination per se, as indicated in a large number of terms or symbols for a large number of items. Thus, a society can have an elaborated set of symbols distinguishing among kin, kinds of weather, or ages of animals. Such distinctions, however, express little generality in that there are unique symbols for each category, each of which must be known. The underlying dimensions, or the basis of classification, are not expressed. For any social system there is a limit to the number of active symbolic categories in use, and, thus, without generalization, there is an upper limit to the variety that can be expressed. Without an increase in the number of labels, by either creating or importing them, development without further generalization will be either slowed down or stopped.[2]

Second, there is a number of statistical regularities or historically founded empirical laws. Such connections in time tend to be recursive regularities. The fundamental characteristic of such generalizations are simple two or three factor connections that are circumscribed by time and place.[3] Again, such connections, although demonstrating commonality in before and after terms, are strictly limited in number—a few thousand such may be the limit of their active use by any society. Such empirical generalizations provide for limited predictions as most statistical generalizations are independent of others.

Third, there are generalizations that are more or less strictly ordered in a hierarchical fashion such that knowing a few will enable the derivation of a number of others. Furthermore, the higher the level of generalization the greater the number of items of variety that can be encompassed by a few general statements.

Such types of generalizations enable almost unlimited amounts of variety to be expressed without approaching the hypothesized upper limits. Such continuous absorption of variety and diversity in the symbol system including that generated by generalization itself, is dependent on the creation of new concepts of generality. In their most structured form, such developmental generalizations are found in the abstract sciences, which can cover with a few statements, in some instances, certain classes of variety everywhere and for all times. In empirical terms, the continued development of highly developed systems depends on the growth of abstract sciences.

The complexity of the symbol system itself becomes organized by the social system. Specialized organizations handle the symbol system reducing complexity for communication, thus providing access.

The conservation of variety is the most immediate consequence of increases in standardization and generalization. With generalization it is possible to retain information about the variety. Since generalizations are hierarchically ordered in terms of complexity, it is possible to reproduce symbols of properties at lower levels of complexity that are expressed in symbols at higher levels.

The higher the level of development, the higher the level of generalization in the symbol system. Thus, not only does a higher level of development enable an increase in the production of new variety but it also enables the recovery, through symbolic manipulation, of all past variety.

Predictability

Prediction is a cognitive act by which information is derived from one or more observations about something not observed. It includes both prediction in the future and postdiction or explanation of past events. Increases in rationalization, generalization, and standardization of the symbol systems lead to increased capacity to predict, both of components and of the system as a whole.

Rationalization, expressing relationships among the properties of the components of the system, leads to prediction in terms of cognitive linkages with the social system which are inclusive, enabling connections to be made with a higher proportion of the total number of components and properties. Standardization, expressing common units, enables moving from one property to other properties with known consequences.

Generalization and discrimination affect predictability in two basic ways. First, there is the accuracy of the predictions derived from having smaller and smaller units to predict. Thus, instead of predicting the state of the market as a whole, different aspects of the market, such as types of products, are predicted. Second, there is prediction across time and space. It enables inferences from observations to things not yet experienced.

The greater the number of the units of information, the smaller those units—which are more precisely refined in terms of discrimination—and the more accurate the predictions. Although statistical laws (such as the market change in prices following changes in money) may provide for more accuracy than structured generalizations, they do so at the loss of scope and ease of prediction. But as development proceeds, predictability in terms of both accuracy and generality will increase.

Predictability is reduced with the introduction of new variety. An item is not yet integrated—its connections are yet to be expressed—and thus the scope of predictions is proportionally reduced. When variety is translated into diversity, there is again a reduction in predictability. With integration of diversity and the establishment of connections among components, predictability is increased, depending on the extent to which that diversity is rationalized, generalized, and standardized.

Because there are iterative interactions between generalization and actual diversity, there often is a trade-off between predictability in terms of scope and accuracy. For example, in specific branches of sciences, new observations contribute to an increase in available data and to understanding variation. Later on, these observations of diversity become integrated (or some of them do) with theoretical discoveries. Increasing the level of generality for existing variety often occurs at the cost of accuracy in prediction. With development, however, the time interval of the trade-off becomes shortened. Thus, at a low levels of development, generalization about variety may come after a long period of time, but as the total level of generality is increased, this time interval is shortened to a point where discrimination and generalization can take place at almost instantaneous time. The time interval will depend on the nature of available languages of generality, some of which will be highly abstract, like mathematical languages that can be used for a large range of empirical phenomena.

At relatively high levels of integrated diversity, where the predictability of the system is high, it becomes possible to predict the emergence of new variety. Thus, what is theoretically possible and technically likely can be anticipated. The emergence of variety is less likely to happen as a random event.

If a property is known to be possible, it can be selected in preference to existing variety. Such predictions make it possible to choose variety that does not exist but is likely to contribute most to, to be most easily integrated into, existing diversity. Predictability of new variety, although never completely certain, for systems to respond to new variety as if they already existed, thus shortening the time taken to integrate new variety. The speed of integrating new variety is increased to the extent that new variety is predicted.

The critical role of prediction in developmental change lies in symbolic manipulations of interactions and transactions. Exchanges can take place across a wider range of units; responses of other components can be anticipated with less cost and greater accuracy; the timing of activities can be made precise in terms of knowledge of the point in time that other components are likely to have properties to exchange; fluctuations can be minimized as a result of a larger number of items of variety and knowledge about alternative locations of properties. The most general way to characterize the predictability of transaction systems is to note the merger of communication and information.

The Relationship Among the Cognitive Processes

Once it is linked to the changing structure of developmental systems, the symbol system takes on certain characteristics of developmental processes. Rationalization, standardization, and generalization are characteristics of the symbols. They are structurally similar to inclusiveness, extensiveness, and relatedness of integration on the one hand, and to diversity on the other. They are processes in that they change along with changes in the social structure. First, there is rationalization which identifies diversity and expresses relationships among properties and components.

Second, there is generalization and discrimination which organize diversity, on the one hand, and express increasing differences among properties and among components, including the deaggregation of components, on the other. Third, there is standardization in which characteristics of the components are expressed in common languages, such that each property of each component can be compared to other properties of other components. These can be likened to an ordered data matrix that is accurate and inclusive, to an interchangeable measurement language of standard intervals of difference, and to generalized relationships which, although few in number, are able to reproduce all of the relationships present in the data matrix.

The developmental basis of rationalization and standardization is the level and rate of development. With few items of diversity to connect, or mostly similarities, there is little rationalization. With little diversity and similarity, there is little to generalize about—generalization takes the form of statistical regularities rather than statements about variance. With few similarities, there is little basis to standardize—simple names or proper names are sufficient to name cases or classes of cases. With development and increasing variety and diversity, the foundation for the cognitive process of the symbol system becomes directly related to what there is to rationalize, standardize, and generalize about.

As was indicated, the more properties that are standardized and the greater the linkages in terms of generalization, the greater are the possibilities for recognizing diminishing differences among properties as well as their similarities. The generalized categories enable more and more discrimination among properties, increasing the total number of properties that can become diversity, linking it through generalization. Generalization is both the response to diversity and the basis for additional diversity.

The consequence of increases in each of these, rationalization, standardization, and generalization, is greater predictability. Predictability is an obvious cognitive requisite for integration: it is definitionally identical to reduction in the randomness of the system. Predictability, as a general property of the system, increases and decreases in tandem with the processes of integrating diversity.

Implications for Development

Predictability contributes to integrative behavior in several related ways. First, there are the reduced costs of knowing places in systems where exchanges can be effectuated or identifying properties can have an impact on transition systems. Second, because of increased differences that are recognized, there is increased sensitivity and responsiveness resulting from increases in selectivity that prediction provides. Third, with development there is less disturbance from new variety in terms of reducing integration, because new variety can be anticipated. Fourth, with generalization, leading to inclusion of properties that are defined as relevant, a critical part of integrating diversity, several cognitive barriers to integration are reduced. Such a result has been designated as secularization. Fifth, the cognitive processes increase the absorptive capacity of the system to absorb new variety. This speaks to the upper limits of active symbols that can be used by a society. The structure of the cognitive processes allows for new items of variety to be taken into the cognitive structure rather than to be grouped with existing categories or to be rejected and not used.

In addition to the specific relationships between developmental cognitive processes and further development that have been suggested, there are two general implications for development—the assumptions of the conservation of variety and the stability of the system.

The conservation of variety stems from greater generalization allowing more variety to be expressed in the symbols. All previous variety that is not active can be related to the active variety. Distinctions can be made between previous variety, active variety, and predicted variety. The cognitive processes, in addition to enabling prediction of new variety, provide a way of keeping all previous variety, some of which from time to time may be reactivated. But with development and these cognitive processes, the total amount of variety contained in the symbol system increases more rapidly than the active variety. In most coaction systems the available variety and the active variety are about equal; with development, the active variety as a proportion of total available variety continually declines.

The conservation of variety is manifest in temporal consciousness in terms of the system's symbols. The issue is simply not past, present, or future orientation but the scope of time that is coded in the symbol system. Highly developed systems will thus be past, present, and future oriented, spanning all time in their symbol centers. Less developed systems will not only have short memories, or if long, rather undifferentiated in specific time intervals, but will also have little future orientation. Regardless of attitudinal predispositions, the symbol system is not capable of maintaining and expressing all of the potentially available variety from the past. Again, despite the fact that the total active variety of highly developed systems is a declining proportion of the total available, the total amount of active variety is continually increasing.

The second major consequence of predictability deriving from the cognitive processes concerns fluctuations of the system.[4] With development, changes in the system make less of a total impact on the system as a whole. The stabilizing effects of these cognitive processes are due to several factors, some of which have been suggested. First, there is the capability to anticipate new variety and adapt to it in advance of it actually occurring. Such anticipatory responses reduce the time during which new diversity reduces integration. Second, along with these cognitive processes there are alternative properties or combinations of properties that become interchangeable for any property, especially as these properties are expressed in standardized units. Thus, losses in one area through consumption or decay can not only be replaced but compensated for in multiple ways and in a short period of time. Third, there is a substantial amount of stored or available variety, such that any old variety that would add to development can be called into use. The development effects of reactivated old variety will be better known than those of new. Fifth, with increased knowledge, the destabilizing effects of interactions and transactions will be reduced as sensitivity to small differences will reduce the probability of overresponding to change. Thus the responses of systems will tend to fit precisely the amount of deviance rather than lead to destabilization by overreacting.[5]

The cognitive processes lead to an ever increasing amount of variety, its recognition as well as its predictability, which is the foundation for integrative behavior. Indeed, at some point in development the set of symbols that represents the system will be a highly integrated information system.

NOTES

1. This discussion uses some of the forms of functionalism. Again, functional explanations are not appropriate for developmental systems. They do have relevance for co-action systems whose study was in part responsible for the discovery of functional concepts and their application.

2. In importing new technology countries also import the symbols describing it.

3. Examples are supply and demand, action and reaction, etc. These combine a generalization with a concept.

4. Again it should be emphasized that development is not a smooth, stable process, but requires destroying certain components in order to occur.

5. Some of these notions are well developed in control systems theory, where the responses of the system are calibrated precisely to changes in stimulus inputs in comparison with crude or undifferentiated responses to any kind of changes in stimulus inputs.

Chapter 7

MANIFESTATIONS OF

DEVELOPMENTAL CHANGE

In this century development has been primarily described as industrialization, urbanization, and mechanization. These are seen as basic to development, producing economic surpluses by increasing economic output per capita and leading to other developmental manifestations, such as social mobility, markets, and "free" labor.

Development has also been specifically identified with a more concrete range of social phenomena—literacy, telephones, newspapers, roads, water supply, electricity, sewage. These are specific means of linking households and individuals to the system. Such fundamental linkages have to a large extent dominated contemporary policy discussions of development; they are specific historical developmental phenomena; both consequences and causes of developmental processes.

The study of a limited range of developmental phenomena cannot provide a sound theoretical framework for understanding developmental change. Such phenomena are not monotonically tied to the basic, underlying dynamics of developmental change—

variety, diversity, similarity, and the integration of diversity. Telephones, for example, may contribute in one context to a rapid increase in diversity by bringing together existing variety that is highly geographically dispersed. In other contexts, telephones may primarily contribute to similarities. Under some conditions, telephones may contribute equally to similarity and diversity. Indeed, since telephones are largely interaction communication—primarily two-way—their use may dampen development of transaction networks.

Identifying development with specific sets of historical phenomena, of course, limits generality. If the gross national product, which is largely based on exchanges of object properties, ceases to increase or even declines, it cannot be concluded that development has also stopped. Indeed, development may be rapidly increasing in terms of transactions of properties proper, improving the quality of life. It may even be that some highly industrialized countries are now in a situation of trading off GNP growth for increased development. At low levels of development, variety may be introduced through the production or import of new products adding to variety, but there is little capacity either to distribute that variety and generate diversity or to integrate existing diversity.

Urbanization is one way of aggregating diversity. The "wealth of cities" is the agglomeration of variety and the provision of cheap access to it. But whether or not urbanization is developmental depends on available alternative technologies for interactions and transactions. National urban centers, for example, may have lost their developmental thrust because of rationalization, standardization, and extension of communication technology. Cities as components of great variety within highly developed countries, attracting variety from the whole nation, may now be in the process of shifting their activities to a global system, leaving the least developed components within them to decay. Cities in less developed countries may be aggregating similarity —poor people with about equal skills—rather than aggregating variety. They may be population aggregations rather than aggregations of diversity that contribute to the processes of developmental change.

Thus, specific social phenomena must be interpreted within the context of specific empirical systems—localities, regions, countries, or global systems—in terms of both their historical peculiarities and their general level of development.

There are, however, some general manifestations of development that are more or less monotonically related to increasing levels of development and are tied to the nature of the system—interaction or transaction systems. Four of these will be discussed: socialization and individualization, differentiation and specialization, equality and inequality, and conflict and cooperation.

Socialization and Individualization

One of the central system dynamics used in this analysis is cross-level interaction. Higher levels emerge and affect lower levels. These lower levels, in turn, become different kinds of system components. The laws of aggregative diversity and inclusive similarity and of the attractiveness of variety are examples. Socialization of activities and individualization are manifestations of this dynamic of levels. Rather than competing processes, they are complementary: an increase in one leads to an increase in the other over time.

Socialization parallels the process of integrating individuals and groups into the system. As socialization increases, an increasing proportion of an increasing number of properties of components become linked to an increasing number of other components, intermediate structures, and the system itself. For individuals this means that food, shelter, health, and other basic needs become linked to social structures, and the number of such properties and activities that become so linked increase with an increase in the total number of properties. Accordingly, social structures and organizations become increasingly differentiated.

Along with socialization, the individual becomes more differentiated in terms of his variety, acquiring more autonomy to select among an increasing number of alternatives. As his properties increase and as the number of potential linkages to other components increase, the individual acquires more autonomy. Thus, with increasing interdependence there is increasing dependence on any one aspect or part of the system. Dependence is in effect reduced by expanding the alternatives which increase with interdependence; no single structural linkage can decisively matter. Such interdependence, however, means neither self-sufficiency nor the possibility of withdrawal from the system. Individualization comes from the system and is related to its level of development. Instead of dependence on any part of the system, there is total dependence on the whole system. Individualization occurs because of the scale of the system, and one consequence of scale is capacity to absorb any kind of individual differences.

With development and socialization and individualization, individual activities are increasingly transferred to the system, increasing the scale of the system and decreasing the individual's dependence on smaller scale subunits of the system. This shift to the system occurs because of the assumption of upper limits and the law of attractiveness of variety. The individual, accordingly, is limited in the amount of variety he can hold by this "biological" limit. But with development and socialization of existing properties, the individual can "have" the freedom to choose among all properties through the access provided by the system.

Variety is necessary for individualization. With similarities alone the individual cannot be distinguished from others and cannot be differentiated in structures of interdependence. The requisites for individualization are differences for the individual and diversity for the system.

Differentiation and Specialization

The consequences of socialization and individualization are differentiation both of the social structures and of individuals. This differentiation occurs because of the transfer of component similarities to the system as a whole, while it retains, at the component level, those properties that yield diversity. Those properties that are most similar are among the first to be transferred away from the component; the similarity is retained through access, and with the acquisition of additional properties by the components there are increments in total diversity. These transfers break existing social units (which are defined in terms of some similarities) into smaller components, to the point that only individuals remain.

In coaction social systems there are no or minimal individual differences. Those differences that do obtain relate to reproduction and growth. Similarities dominate, and there is no basis for differentiation.

Once a system begins to develop, there is differentiation based on the acquisition of new properties and the processes that integrate them. Such differentiation takes place first among large units and then, increasingly, among smaller ones. What is of primary interest are those structures, organizations, and behaviors that reflect the most recent forms of differentiation.

One kind of differentiation is the emergence of general sectors of behavior (economic, social, political) that themselves become integrated. Structures and behavior become crudely differentiated in terms of classes of activities—social, economic, and political being the most frequently identified. Prior to such differentiation, political, economic, and social behavior cannot be identified with separate structures. With some development of the system and some differentiation, it is proper to speak of social, economic, and political development. The differentiation at these microstructures is based on differentiation at other microlevels within the system. At the initial stages of such differentiation, social institutions dominate economic activities, and economic institutions are clearly mixed with, often controlling, political ones.

Following a general, crude differentiation of sectors, what follows are specialized institutions within each sector, for example, politics and administration, production and trade, and groups and associations. With increased differentiation and specialization these sectors continue to specialize at different rates, often leading to conflict not only among but also within them.

The emergence of a developmental system from a coaction society, where similarities predominate and production is intrinsic, brings about a fundamental cleavage between those elements of the society that become part of developmental processes and those that remain primarily in the historical coaction system. According to the definition of a developmental system, such coaction "system" groups are not members of the system, although they may share cultural similarities, inhabit the same territory, provide a source of people, and act as a safety valve for individuals failing in the developmental system. The relationship between an emerging developmental system founded in an environment of a coaction system is one of societal cleavage that has little initial direct bearing on the structure and processes of the development except insofar as the developmental system will begin to expand and penetrate it. The cleavage between the two is one of near discontinuity. Such a cleavage differs from those where there are some relationships between the two, even though not reciprocal, such as dominance.

Equality and Inequality

Equality and inequality are generally consequences of development, and a direct consequence of the differentiation resulting from development. There are several dimensions of equality, each of which depends on the nature of the system. First, there is equality in terms of identities, which is characteristic of coaction systems. Each "individual" has properties more or less identical to every other. Second, there is quantitative equality in terms of the number of properties of both similarities and differences. Components will have many of the same properties and some that are different. Equality will be defined as having the same amount of the same property. If variety and the total properties are limited, there will be substantial inequality in the number of properties of components as well as in the relevance of those properties. Third, there is equality in terms of the variety of properties, assuming the total number is relatively equal among components. In transaction systems, there will be increasing equality among components both in properties (approaching the individual's upper limit) and in the unique combination of the variety of those properties. In all three cases, equality is a generalized, aggregative relational property of a system.

In systems at a low level of development there is substantial social inequality both in the number and kinds of properties. The inequality of a system is derivable from the number of properties and number of components and the kinds of properties they have. If these properties are few in number and variety, inequalities are categoric, that is, identifiable by groupings of components on a few differences. There are components with many properties and those with a few, those with one kind and those with another—

e.g., landowners and tenants. Three of four basic categories of differences, both quantitative and qualitative unfold, forming social strata and classes.

With increases in the total number of properties and consequent differentiation, not only does the number of categories of components begin to increase, but also the categories within categories. As activities become sectorized, different types of inequalities emerge. But insofar as these categories are limited, a few continue to dominate the pattern of inequality. Occupation, for example, may predict most of the inequality in other properties when the total number of categories is small, and a diminishing amount when the number of categories increases.

Because of the limited number of properties and variety, and because of the relationship between the accumulation of properties and the production of similarities and new variety, some inequality is a structural condition for development. If the limited number of existing properties were, in other words, equally distributed, then the accumulation necessary for increasing production would be less than sufficient to maintain an increasing rate of development. With a limited number of properties, the greater the inequality (up to some limit that would stagnate development), the higher the level of development. Of course, certain levels or configurations of inequality would stop exchanges or would actually reduce the level of development. In interaction systems, the lower the level of development, the greater the equality; with some development there is increasing inequality; with still more development, greater equality. Equality-inequality is both a cause and consequence of development.

Conflict and Cooperation

Development leads to differentiation; differentiation results in inequality; inequality creates the conditions for conflict. Conflict is behavior that leads to a distribution of properties either without the consent or against the "interests" of the components. In discussing developmental manifestations, choice and interest become appropriate concerns, although they are difficult to assess and will not be defined here.

Depending on a number of factors, such as consciousness of inequality and strong participatory institutions, there will be demand for the distribution of properties. This follows from the assumption of component preference for variety and the consequent enhancement of the component's significance in the system. Thus the structure of conflict deriving from inequalities will turn into conflict. Underlying interaction systems is exchange or cooperation, or on the other end of the continuum, conflict, where the movement of properties leaves one component perceptibly better or worse off than others.

These conflict structures are the conditions for politics and government, which will (1) influence the distribution of properties, either directly or indirectly; (2) assume the role of regulator of accumulation and production; or (3) manage demand for redistribution, including suppressing it. If, of course, there is an abundance of properties and variety, inequality would diminish to a point where conflict, and thus political management of conflict, would recede.

At low levels of development demand for redistribution will be minimal; with some level of development and an immediate past history of an increase in development, demand will increase. As demand for properties increases, so does the capacity of organizations to obtain additional properties. Those actors that have just received more properties than they have had at some previous point in time will not only demand more but will actually be able to secure more. As a consequence, overall inequalities will increase.

For most political systems there is a crisis at the conjunction of increased properties and increasing inequality. Responses can include distribution, leading to the consequence of accelerating demand by those who have received the most in proportion to their immediate past; the suppression of demand, leading to the consequence of less overall exchange or transfer of properties, with the added consequence of a lower rate of development, or of stagnation; or the shifting of the context of conflict to institutions able to manage it, with the consequence of incorporating distribution and/or production into the state with the capacity to coerce.

Without governmental intervention in the face of development and increasing inequality, distribution by overt conflict and violence could occur. Demand exceeds the system's capacity for supply, including promises of future properties. The demand is likely to be highest among those who have just entered the system and are beginning to become part of the developmental process. As the properties are few, few components have many, and many components have few. A redistribution, by overt conflict, would turn the system around, a revolution. The consequences could either be a distribution of properties insufficient for increased production, including that of new properties, or a new distribution that would rapidly accelerate development.

Cooperation is a form of interaction in which each of the cooperating parties is better off, or they are all better off together. Cooperation can be viewed as one end of a cooperation-exchange-conflict continuum. Conditions for cooperation in interaction systems would be a positive rate of development, including anticipated development, in excess of the rate of increases in demand. Widespread cooperation would further the conditions for the transformation of interaction systems into transaction ones, where properties proper are not scarce and are not located in unique places in time and space. Whatever remnants of competition and conflict remain would recede into irrelevancy.

EPILOGUE

This volume has been theoretical. There are no systematic applications of the theory to specific problems or cases. There are hints of what some applications might look like.

It is our view that macrotheories with such a diversity of potential applications are not confirmed or disconfirmed by one or even many studies in the social sciences, where the historical and contextual variances are so great. Rather, confirmation is built first by the accumulation of studies found to be consistent with theoretical expectations and then the organization of these studies into a structure of confirmation, an organized set of data generated by the theory that explicitly states additional expectations.

We have examined some classes of data—increases over time in trade flows from the most developed regions within a country (holding constant political and legal barriers to trade) to the more highly developed countries (law of attractiveness of variety); patterns of local explanations of change giving way to regional level explanations as the developmental level of the region increases (shifts in levels); differences in preference for governmental redistributional policies under different levels of regional development; demands for redistribution; and the differentiation of sectors as a function of the level of development (differentiation).

Other studies tend to yield findings that are in line with this theory: (1) a shift of values from material (object properties) to nonmaterial (properties proper) values with higher levels of development; (2) a loosening of party identification based on similarities with development among the most highly developed individuals (the educated) within the most developed countries resulting in a decline in intermediate structures); (3) patterns of population concentration in countries recently becoming developed or industrialized; and (4) dispersion of both people and activities in highly developed countries where linkages among individuals are being established through communication networks rather than physical proximity (shifts from production of object properties to properties proper). These are but a few of the phenomena that are being included in an inventory of confirmatory studies.

Certainly we are theoretically biased and we do ignore disconfirming cases. But we believe that the weight of the evidence does and will provide credibility to, if not convincing confirmation of, this theory as against others. Since the theory is general, the potential number of relevant studies is almost without limit.

We will both independently apply this theory to specific problems where these very general abstract developmental laws will take shape in concrete cases. In particular, what will be addressed are the conflicts between the subjective forces for change and those for maintaining the status quo in the contemporary world.